Dedicated to Ranchers who understand the need for humor

"Do you, Rachel, take Ranching for Better or for Worse?"

by Rachel Carr Klippenstein

Rood Bridge Publishing

HILLSBORO, OREGON

Rood Bridge Publishing
Post Office Box 1322
Hillsboro, OR 97123

Klippenstein, Rachel Carr, 1942-
"Do you, Rachel, take Ranching for Better or for Worse?"
Ranching/Humor
p. cm.
1. Klippenstein, Rachel Carr—essays 2. Ranch life—Pennsylvania. 3. Ranch life—
South Dakota. 4. Ranch life—Oregon.

ISBN 0-9647709-2-X

Printed in the United States of America

Design by Becky Gyes
Illustrations by Larry Davis

Acknowledgements

Weekend mornings when I sit at the computer, the hours slip by as though time didn't exist, like a rancher when he's out checking the calving pasture.

Months pass. As the calves grow in substance, so does the manuscript. Weaning soon separates the young from their mothers. The young bulls and heifers will be on their own. They will have to fend for themselves. Neighboring ranchers will inspect them. "It's a good calf—strong top line, stands square on her legs, but I'd like to lengthen her neck a little and see more muscle expression in her hindquarters."

Returning to the computer room, I approach the seventh draft of the book with the zeal of a protective mother cow. I don't want any weak quarters. I persevere, satisfied I've given this project my best efforts. Then comes the frightening period of separation.

I'm proud of the "calf" I've raised, but unsure about my readiness to wean myself from what I've given birth to. Can I accept constructive criticism from those whose opinions I respect, yet know I'll be intimidated by?

To successfully breed cattle, we ranchers depend on the honest appraisal of our fellow breeders. We listen. We want our product to meet the demands of those who purchase our breeding stock. We absorb all the information we can, as we strive to achieve perfection.

I acknowledge and thank those who participated in the betterment of *"Do you Rachel, take Ranching for Better or for Worse?"*

Husband • Sons • Mothers • Fathers • Brothers • Sisters • Aunts Uncles • Cousins • Inlaws • Outlaws • Friends • Creative Writing Instructor, George Staley • Mentor and editor, Myrna Oakley Writers at all stages of development • Readers • Editors • Listeners Naysayers • Proof Readers • Computer Specialists • Artists Dreamers

Table of Contents

Prologue

A

B

C

D

F

G

H

I

J

Prologue

City girl turns country woman

As a young girl growing up in Pittsburgh, I did what other city kids did. I roller skated to and from friends' houses, rode the bus to school and walked to the Manor Movie Theater where we sat through five hours of cartoons for two bits apiece.

My brothers and I saved our allowances to buy fifty-cent tickets to the Peanut Gallery at Forbes Field, home of the Pittsburgh Pirates baseball team. So few spectators showed up during the long, hot, losing summers, that by the third inning we were cheering our team from the box seats.

On rainy days, we stalked Greek columns and stared at nude sculptures in the Carnegie Museum. We also stared wide-eyed at the enormous paintings, the art that hung in dark halls. After our romp through the museum, we slipped into the Carnegie Library next door where we spent hours exploring hundreds of shelves of books before choosing our monthly allotment of titles.

During the cold, gray days in January and February, we ice-skated on small frozen ponds or zoomed down the steep, snow-packed Cemetery Hill on our American Flyer sleds. When our hands and feet were frozen, we slipped back through the bent bar in the wrought-iron fence, just a few yards from Nina's house, where her mother always had hot chocolate waiting for us.

Pittsburgh offered many activities that appealed to a child. A summer playground at Whightman Elementary School, where I dazzled ping pong opponents with my spinning serve. Or licking an orange Creamsicle outside Doc's Drug Store after an intense half hour flipping baseball trading cards.

But it was that one day every summer when our family attended the Allegheny County Fair that most captivated my imagination. The minute we walked through the turnstiles, I was immediately drawn to the livestock area—like an actress drawn to the stage.

I walked back and forth along aisles of haltered cattle and stalls where sleek, beautiful horses were penned. I watched moms and dads and kids tend their livestock. They looked like they were having a good time washing and brushing their animals. The hay smelled sweeter than cotton candy.

While my three brothers were off scaring themselves on the carnival rides or losing money to hawkers at the games of chance, I was content to watch the cattle owners present their groomed and polished animals to the judge in the livestock show ring. I was enthralled by the drama of it—and I wanted to be one of the cast members.

Although I had no idea why the judge placed one animal over another, it was enough to hear the spectators cheer or groan as they witnessed the judge's decisions. But restlessness grew within me. Somehow I had to find a way out of the concrete city to the open spaces of the country.

At the age of ten, I began plotting my escape to the country. I bought a western shirt at the Goodwill store, complete with pearl snaps. I scrounged a straw cowboy hat from the same place. And I finally convinced my parents that I really needed a pair of cowboy boots for my eleventh birthday.

I sensed my mother's distress when she walked into my bedroom and saw me standing in front of the dresser mirror admiring myself in my new cowgirl outfit. "A phase," I heard her say as she walked from the room. I smiled. I never did like wearing dresses.

At the library, I read books about cattle. As an eighth grader, I even wrote a research paper on feeding bulls in Montana. I didn't understand that a steer wasn't born a steer. I secretly planned to enroll at Penn State University's agricultural school.

When puberty dealt me its surprises, I momentarily strayed from my desire to enter the College of Agriculture. Especially when a dark-haired boy asked me to go for a ride in his brand new red convertible. As we sped along narrow city streets, I thrilled at the maple trees with their new leaves and the fresh smell of newly mown grass.

I was nearly persuaded to give up my dream by the distraction of masculine good looks and the freedom offered in the jazzy red convertible. But the nagging image of wide-open spaces and cattle made me realize I couldn't spend a lifetime with a person whose only interest was the upkeep of a 1954 Chevrolet. He had no aspirations. No direction. No dreams.

Right then and there, I decided I would look for a fellow cowboy—one with whom I could share my cattle dream. I drew a mental picture of my perfect life-partner so I'd know when I met him that he was the one. He would be close to six feet tall, but not much more because I was just over five feet. He would have a muscular torso, with long arms dangling at his sides.

I imagined this perfect specimen would have blond hair clipped in a short crew cut. He would be an athlete who excelled in his chosen sport, his sky blue eyes challenging every opponent. My cowboy would have prominent cheek bones, and he would reveal a playfulness that hid an obsessive ability to work very hard.

Two years later, as a junior in high school, my parents drove me three hundred miles to a church boarding school, fifteen miles east of Philadelphia. Dejected and homesick after six weeks, I sat unhappily on the sidelines of my first high school dance. I stared uncomfortably at my peers, a noisy crowd of awkward teenagers milling about in the decorated basketball court. I was wishing I could slip outside to call Dad to drive down and rescue me, when I glanced toward the door. And there he was! A serious-looking, blond- haired, skinny guy. And he was walking towards me. I smoothed the stiff bow on my yellow taffeta dress.

Hi," he said. "My name's Marc."

I blushed.

"Do you wanna dance?" He beckoned with the largest hand I'd ever seen. The long arms startled me. He wore a snappy blue sports coat. And had an impeccable crew cut.

"Sure," I stammered.

He guided me around the dance floor with grace, his large hand firmly directing our movements. Could life be better? I could hardly breathe. Here was a real cowboy, I was sure.

Marc lived on a small farm a half a mile from the campus. We dated five years before agreeing on the commitment of marriage. They were five years filled with answers to my cowgirl yearnings. I got to practice being a cowgirl! I helped push calves toward their expectant mamas. I helped bed the barn with bright golden wheat straw.

Many warm spring afternoons I sat atop the board rail corral fence watching my cowboy lunge his colt in preparation for a horse show. And on cool, damp evenings we sat on a hay bale in the barn waiting and watching for his mare to give birth to a gangly, energetic foal. Another time, when I cut my hand on the barbed wire fence, Marc rushed me to the Emergency Room of Holy Redeemer Hospital in nearby Rockledge. I was so proud of my seven stitches.

There were the hot, summer mornings we led Marc's 4-H steer to the end of the long dirt driveway and back, hardening its muscles in preparation for the livestock show in Harrisburg.

I stood in tense anticipation as my cowboy, dressed in new Levis, a brown and black plaid western shirt and a straw cowboy hat, led his well-groomed steer into the arena to be judged. I could barely contain my excitement when the judge nodded for Marc to lead his steer out from the fifty animals standing nose to tail around the ring.

And then the gut-wrenching disappointment as the judge made his final placings. Third place. All the washing and brushing! And the miles of walking to firm up the animal's muscles and work off the fat. The sadness in Marc's eyes made me think about Chevy convertibles and the city life. But, not for long.

"Are you sure this is the kind of life you want?" Mom asked.

"Yes," I replied. "There'll be another show and another judge.

There'll be another steer. You should see the calf Marc's already picked out for next year. He's not even weaned from his mother yet, but he'll be a great one. I'm sure of it."

With child-like abandonment, I eagerly entered marriage and the world of cattle in Huntingdon Valley, Pennsylvania, five miles from the school where we first met. I was barely twenty-one years old. It was here in our two-hundred-year-old stone house, that I learned to cook for appetites that far exceeded any I had witnessed growing up with three brothers. I learned that a steaming pot of spaghetti wasn't Marc's idea of lunch for the haying crew on a 94-degree afternoon.

And weather took on new significance, different than when I was a kid watching from the living room window as the Big Snow of 1952 piled up higher and higher on the cobblestones of Beelermont Place. School that year closed for three days. My brothers and I built snow igloos and wore ourselves out pulling sleds up our dead end street for the fast rides down.

I couldn't have imagined then that twenty years later I would move to South Dakota with my husband and our two sons. Or that I'd be slogging through three-foot snow drifts in sub-zero temperatures to treat a bull calf weakened from diarrhea, praying he would live through the minus ten degree night.

My perspective of time changed from the day-to-day familiar routine of childhood experience to the throbbing pulse of ranching. I learned that seasons, more than Mondays and Tuesdays, marked a rancher's existence. That the animals determined whether or not we were able to attend holiday functions. I learned that cows aren't particular when they decide to calve or get sick.

I loved the expansive South Dakota grassland, despite its unforgiving nature. Emotions here stirred unlike any I had felt during my city years. As a young teen, I had cried when Sandy, my cocker spaniel, ran into the street and got caught under the wheels of a car, leaving me to bottle feed her five two-week old puppies. I even bawled when my yellow parakeet died.

But those tears were a trickle compared to the wrenching sobs that came at the end of a 10-day vigil at the side of a herd bull ravaged by rabies. And more tears of frustration when a month-old heifer calf, full of potential, succumbed to internal scours. These were cries from deep within my heart and soul.

Nor could the fourteen-year-old girl who was thrilled that her orphan pups survived, have anticipated the immense joy she would experience at a newborn calf's measured breaths following a difficult delivery. Or the wild ecstacy this woman—me—would feel as a grown-up, when the judge presented us the championship banner for best pen of three bulls one year at the National Western Stock Show in Denver.

In addition to satisfying huge appetites, enduring extreme weather conditions and dealing with fluctuating emotions, I learned one more lesson. It was about money. The significance of dollars and cents. I learned that not having enough money in the bank could overshadow a vibrant summer sunset or the beauty of a lush, green South Dakota prairie. The little girl who once budgeted her baby sitting earnings into a half-a-dozen envelopes, grew into a woman who stared at too many envelopes with never enough money to fill even one. Over the years, hundreds of thousands of dollars were traded for cattle with the Lazy H brand. But there was rarely enough cash to keep pace with the high cost of doing business.

I also learned one other important lesson. That highs and lows and everydays are met with a strong faith in the future. A gut-feeling that God is there. Humor is the armor He gives us to withstand the great sadnesses, as well as the overpowering happy moments. Learning the gift of laughter helps put life in perspective.

Much has been written about the dark side of life. About struggles in an unfair society where to be rich with dollars and cents is prized above a treasure chest rich with the memories of taking part. In the doing—not in the spectating.

But I think laughter is even more appreciated because of the difficult journey. How frightened I was when I first saw our oldest cow, Martha, on her back in the old bathtub that served as a watering hole. Her eyes were rolled back. Her breathing was labored. We hurried and brought the tractor and chain to right her. Then there was relieved and loud laughter when we realized that she would be alright. Snap. A picture was captured in our minds, to be reviewed later when the seriousness of life threatened our ability to cope.

In this alphabetic album of snapshots and essays, I endeavor to share stories of my life on a ranch. Listed alphabetically, you can quickly sort through to the subject areas you are most curious about. Be it thoughts on alfalfa, bugs and bulls or on goosenecks, loans or weather, I hope you will laugh and cry as we explore the question, "Do you, Rachel, take Ranching for Better or for Worse?".

Age/Cattle

Junior or senior?

Even a neophyte can differentiate between spring calves and fall calves. And nearly everyone can follow the conversations about yearlings. But why, I thought, is there a winter calf, yet no winter yearling?

And then there are junior and senior calves and junior and senior yearlings. Early in my training years, Marc and I took four bulls to a spring sale in Ohio. To determine the sale order, all the animals are lined up according to age. As a bull is selected from the front of one of the half-dozen lines, another bull is brought in to replace him.

I eyed the three bulls tied to the arena fence while Marc held the halter of a front line bull. The judge selected Marc's bull. As he led the animal from the line-up, he motioned to me. "Bring the senior calf to the line," he hollered.

I pointed to the bull next to me. "This one?" I mouthed the words, not wanting to shout my ignorance throughout the crowd of bulls and breeders.

Marc turned his head away. "Not that one!" he shouted. "The senior calf." He frowned.

I looked over at the three bulls. One down. Two to choose from. Hot embarrassment flushed my cheeks red. I quickly selected the animal closest to me because I didn't want to push my 110 pounds between the antsy bulls. Bravely, I brought this bull forward, but Marc turned and glared at me. Then he reached over and untied the middle bull.

"You're holding the junior yearling, Rachel. I said calf, senior calf. Can't you figure out a yearling is older than a calf—we only brought one calf." He strode off to place the senior calf in the sale line-up.

15

I looked at the bulls again, thinking age classification can't be that difficult, but also deciding I'd study up on all this age stuff as soon as we got back home.

Age/Humans

Events, not years

Pregnant with our first child, Marc introduced me as "Rachel, a first calf heifer." I rejected the analogy on grounds that there were no similarities, despite my bulging abdomen.

Of course, human and bovine gestations are approximately nine months duration and toward the end of my final trimester I admit I did look like a fat old cow, but that was for *me* to say aloud, not Marc. Nor did I appreciate Marc referring to Darryl as our "spring calf," though I understood this eased the need to remember specific dates.

Marc and I were married in the spring of 1963. Actually the date was March 30, but for years Marc and I alternated between the thirtieth and the thirty-first, because we could never remember which day it was.

Ranchers mark age by events rather than specific dates. For example, my nephew was born two days after the Tri-City Livestock Exhibition opened. I can't remember the exact day but I know it was in January, 1965, the year Mr. Exuberance was named Champion Tri-City Bull.

I celebrated my fortieth birthday the summer we brought in enough hay to last two years. Marc and I toasted our twentieth wedding anniversary on the same day the last calf was born in the spring of 1983. That year our herd calved 102 percent. We had two sets of twins and no calves died. I discovered that exact dates lose significance.

Nor do we lack respect when we mark death by events rather than precise dates. Grampa died toward the end of January, 1967, the year snow covered the ground through the middle of March. We stomped pathways overtop deeply drifted snow to the feed troughs, watering tanks and hay yards. Imagining Grampa now tending flowers in the warmth of Heaven eased our grief.

My Aunt Mildred died in an automobile accident the second week in October, a week after the announcement that the Sage County 4-H livestock judging team had won a trip to the National Western Stock Show in Denver. Aunt Millie coached our children to photograph the animals with their mind's eye so they could "see" the differences as they presented their reasons for how they placed the class. "Let the judge know you see the classes. Believe you're right and don't back down." Not a fall passes that we don't talk about Aunt Mildred's positive influence on our children.

Remembering exact dates wasn't nearly as important as remembering the person. We thought about the weeks Grampa spent teaching our sons to tie knots. We laughed as we remembered Aunt Millie dancing a jig when the judging team won their trip. Events, not dates, strengthen our resolve or remind us of love shared or sorrow halved.

Age/Wisdom

It ought to be simple

The Age of Wisdom is sought by ranchers, as well as by folks from all walks of life. We diligently strive to achieve this age, preferably sooner rather than later. Will we become wise at age forty or fifty? Experience is the diligent teacher—different for each of us.

Just at the moment I say, "Aha, I understand, perseverance, hard work and humor are the elements of wisdom," a storm cloud drops rain on freshly swathed hay, and uncertainty clouds my perspective. Or my family, caught up with cleaning the shop, comes in late for dried-out, well-done steaks, which makes me angry and impatient.

These emotions convince me of the longer journey ahead. Habits repeat themselves. Most of us aren't fast learners. Many of us aren't even sure of the goals we seek.

First, I wish to become wise about the ways of cattle. How they move. What they eat. Where they calve. Second, I wish to increase my knowledge of money. How to produce top selling commercial bulls and where to get the money for our mortgage payment. Finally, after succeeding in those two areas, I plan to devote my life to the wisdom of mankind and how to enhance my friendships.

Then, I realize these goals are congruent, not hierarchal, like steps on the hay mow ladder.

Life is complicated. I want simplicity. I also want financial independence, but I'm not sure what that is. When I stash $10,000 will I be secure? I doubt it. How about $25,000? Maybe. But my friends don't care to wait. They want me as I am now, albeit devoid of money and wisdom. They reassure me that the warts and flaws are okay. They have some, too.

Perhaps the Age of Wisdom isn't the peak of life's mountain. It's a culmination of bits and pieces that Experience teaches us. It's knowing that kindnesses are returned. That joy is in giving. That bird songs brighten our days. That husbands don't always throw their dirty clothes beside the hamper. That once in a while children wash dishes without being asked, or ride out in the early morning to check cattle so Dad can sleep in.

Could it be we experience the Age of Wisdom at the same time we learn the lessons of life? There are so many lessons, we complain. Yet, we meet people who seem at peace. They must be wise. They are there to give us hope in the striving. In the knowing that we, too, will appreciate Experience and one day truly understand wisdom's age.

Alfalfa

Substitute for gambling

Alfalfa is a miracle legume. Its roots stretch to China or wherever the closest moisture lies. The blue-green leaves growing from sturdy stems provide one of the highest protein sources for cattle. It's a miracle that minus forty degrees below zero doesn't kill the plants, nor does 110 degree heat wither these strong survivors. Year after year, ranchers harvest hay with nary a drop of fertilizer because of the plant's innate nitrogen fixing abilities.

Alfalfa is also the rancher's answer to legalized gambling. While we never underestimate alfalfa's faithful production of feed, we often overestimate the odds of a profitable seed crop.

All ranchers believe that one year, perhaps two years in ten, the alfalfa gods will bestow their good will upon us, permitting a seed crop harvest of 300 pounds to the acre. And furthermore, that the supply and demand gods will be in alignment, which means the seed companies' demand can't keep up with the rancher's supply.

Ranchers also pray that the seed buyer won't severely dock the grower for immature seeds or too many weed seeds. And most important, that the amount paid to the rancher will more than equal the amount of the mortgage payment. Or, if our wildest dreams come true, will equal two years' payments.

Unfortunately, the alfalfa gods rarely see fit to give ranchers a break. Gambling with alfalfa seeds isn't for the faint of heart. Many years we earned barely enough money to pay the combining bill. And yet, the gold is right there, ready to be panned. Should we swath a second cutting hay crop or go for the illusive once in ten year bonanza?

Not once did we chose the former. The temptation is too great. "This will be the big year," we say. Marc and I stroll through the field where our eyes feast upon the millions of purple blooms as our nostrils absorb the sweet fragrance permeating the still air. We reach to caress a stem. We take this as a sign, a good omen that in two months time the plants will bend over from the weighty seeds. Yes, we even imagine the potential profit.

"The rains have been timely," I state with confidence. "The alfalfa gods must intend a magnificent seed crop. I know the gods will treat us fairly."

July. August. We silently pay homage to the gods of alfalfa. The dark brown seed pods are plump with tangy smelling seeds.

"This is the best crop ever." Marc speaks aloud during one of our visitations to the field. "Won't it be great not to worry over next year's mortgage payment! We've worked hard. I don't know how an alfalfa reward once in a great while can harm our spiritual welfare or our earthly welfare, either."

"Shh," I say, fearing our words will be mistaken for greed, knowing the gods are well aware of our financial need.

During the second week of September, Marc and I make daily trips to determine swathing day. Please, I think quietly, my fingers crossed, let this be the year. I promise we'll donate a large sum to the church. I won't be selfish to my neighbors ever again, if we could just have this one good crop. Promise.

"We've been lucky so far," Marc pipes up. "No hail. Perfectly timed rains. Tomorrow, we swath." He smiles and puts his long arms around me. "I love you." Betting can be romantic.

We walk hand in hand from the field, in awe of its potential. Both of us thankful for the abundancy.

That evening we toast our hopes to a good harvest, being cautious not to over imbibe and possibly arouse anger in the gods. Nor do we wish to jinx a harvest so near at hand.

Before sleep comes, my mind considers how pleased our sons will be to have brand new school clothes. And Marc, a new pair of western boots. And finally, the perm I've been dreaming about all summer will become a reality. A head full of curls. Curls. Curls. Boots. Curls. Boots.

Today there is a threat of untimely rain. Marc knocks down the towering alfalfa plants with the sharpened cutting blades of the hay mower. The added risk of unwanted moisture pushes his adrenalin to the max. By afternoon the sun shines its warmth on our field. By evening the leaves are shriveling, bringing us closer to the fateful day of combining. Marc's adrenalin subsides to normal.

I marvel at the miracle plant. How it survives its harsh environment. How it gives and gives, never tiring. I look heavenward. A large, large sum to the church, I again promise. We need this crop to stay in business. Cattle prices are low this fall.

In seven days we arrive at the field to the sound of the neighbor's combine. Chug, chug. Black exhaust fuming from the pipe. Slowly, the machine swallows the dying leaves and stems and spits the tiny hard seeds into the hopper. It's a glorious day!

Marc embraces me. We were so close to losing it all two nights ago when the temperature dropped to near freezing.

The pickup springs tighten as we load the eighty pound bags onto the bed. We run our fingers through the seed. Thank you. This is fine seed. We drive two hours to Ulster where the seed buyer awaits to bargain with us for our hard earned crop.

Marc drags a bag to the scale.

"Good weight," the man says. He opens the bag to sift through the seed. "But too many weed seeds. Have to dock you a nickel."

"Ah, come on," Marc says. "There's not that many. Just look at those alfalfa seeds. Some of the best I've ever raised."

"I'll grant you that," the buyer says, his face set in stone. "But you know how it is. I got to clean the weed seeds out. Takes time. And you know, time is money. Give you 68 cents, a dock of 5. Comes to 63. Pretty good I'd say. Go ahead and unload the rest of the bags over there." He points to the board wall next to the scale.

"Sixty-three cents? Are you serious?" My voice raises a notch. "That's damn good seed. You said so yourself. Sixty-three cents. That'll barely cover the cost of production."

"Listen, Rachel. Take it or leave it. Makes no difference to me. We're overloaded with seed from last year. There's not much demand and a heck of a lot of supply. Don't make no nevermind to me if you sell or if you don't. What do you wanna do?"

Whew. That was a mouthful. We unloaded the pickup. We didn't have a place to store the seed for a possible better price next year.

And so it was, that year the alfalfa gods smiled upon us, but the supply and demand gods frowned. "Don't worry," I mumbled. "I'm betting on next year. I'm sure there'll be better demand."

Every year, we play the alfalfa odds. We know our chances are slim to win, but each year the purple flowers bloom, beckoning us to wager one more time. If we work hard, one of these years we'll be rewarded and will keep our promises.

That night we sip wine and clink glasses. "To next year! Yes, here's to next year." Clink.

Animal/Bovine

Just how stupid are they?

Ranchers manage cattle, rather than alternative grass-eating species, because we admire intelligence in animals. We curse their cleverness, yet we are quietly proud of the smart animals. We note that bulls take their job seriously. Never, willingly, do they take a day off from work. Cows are responsible mothers, always protecting their young from threats of coyotes or a river at flood stage.

Being curious creatures and ever on the lookout for greener grass on the other side of the fence, cattle prowl the pasture perimeters. They poke and sniff their sensitive noses along the wire barriers, searching for a fenceline breach to new lands.

One family line of registered cattle, in search of easy access to the lush, green grass growing temptingly close in the section line adjacent to their quarters, regularly paced the fencelines, stopping between poles to shoulder-test for loose wires. With the grace of a lithe ballet dancer, a cow lifts a wobbly wire and squeezes gently through to the other side and its rewards of more abundant feed.

As Marc drove from the pasture where he had repaired an escape route, Miss Marvelous sauntered over to test Marc's fence-mending skills. She wedged her head between two wires until the upper strand rested taut on her neck. Patiently, she moved her neck from side to side with a steady upward pressure until, POP, a staple flew off. Miss Marvelous, along with her attentive three-month-old heifer calf, boldly slipped between the wires to the unpastured section line, where any fool could see the grass IS greener.

Bulls think about their environment, too. Old Improver, our senior herd sire, preferred his breeding plan over ours. In consideration of Improver's old arthritic legs, Marc and I herded prospective mother cows to the corral where we penned Old Improver. Though he reluctantly performed his herd sire duties within the confinement of a corral, he much preferred managing his own breeding program.

Early one morning, we drove to the pasture to check heat cycles. Old Improver, nostrils flared, was striding through the herd, not one sign of stiff, arthritic joints. How he leaped over the stout six-foot corral fence is his secret.

Most cattle know the difference between being driven toward a corral and being driven to a fresh pasture. When they sense 'corral' with shots and branding, they plod, despite our loud cajoling. But when they smell the trail leading to tall grass, they up the gear from plod to gallop. Cattle often choose where they would rather be.

Angry words flew from our eleven-year-old son, Darryl's mouth when he spotted his 4-H heifer wandering about the fairgrounds. She had rubbed her rope halter off. It was no accident. She purposely rubbed against the wood stall until she succeeded in loosening her restraints. "From now on," Darryl whispered in her large hairy ear, "I'm snapping the neck rope on." He scratched her back. "You're pretty smart, aren't you, even though you're making me look stupid."

Animal/Canine

Hunter dog or cow dog?

Norwegian Elkhounds are hunters, not cow dogs.
Cappy spent his first year of life as a city dog, exploring the concrete jungle at the end of a leash. His occasional romps in the city park provided no opportunities to perfect hunting skills.

When Cappy's city masters sought a country home suitable to his size and stamina, we accepted the challenge of transforming him into a cow dog. This, despite the fact that on his first leashless ranch excursion, he chased a group of yearling heifers through a barbed wire gate.

Marc cursed at the top of his lungs, "Dang blasted dog. Stop! You stupid son of a gun! Where the heck do you think you're going? Get your two-bit butt over here now."

After fifteen minutes of us circling and calling, Cappy lost interest in chasing cattle to follow the trenchant ground hog odor which led to a hole in the middle of the pasture. Dirt flew as the elkhound dug for his quarry.

With promises that we could return Cappy if he "didn't work out," we said good-by to the "City Couple."

"I've got work to do," Marc said. "Good luck capturing the dog. You're the one who wanted a dumb mutt. If he chases the heifers again, he's done for."

So, leash in one hand and an open can of dog food in the other, I marched back to the pasture for the bait and switch maneuver. An hour later, Cappy sheepishly slunk towards me and the food. I snatched the choke chain, pulling hard to snap the leash on as he attempted to rear and twist from my grasp.

His 65 pounds of muscle dragged me home where I locked him on the sun porch. Several times a day Cappy and I endured drag-a-thon runs. In three weeks I lost seven pounds, while his disposition remained surly and his energy, endless.

Returning late one afternoon from a hay delivery trip, I heard

loud, insistent barking. I ran to the sun porch door to reassure Cappy that he hadn't been abandoned. "It's okay, boy." His tightly curled tail wagged in welcome. Then I noticed the old couch—the one we used for overflow company.

Torn to shreds. Stuffing gouged from the couch's interior lay scattered all over the floor. Pillows were viciously ripped open, as though the dog had been seeking out a mouse home. "That's it," I said. "Grab your gun, Marc. We're turning the dog loose. If he attacks the cattle, shoot him."

Why had I insisted we provide a home for this adorable, destructive Elkhound?

Marc dropped a 12 gage shotgun shell into the chamber. I armed myself with a large tree limb and the leash. Cappy clawed at the door, anxious to escape. I shoved the door open and stood back. Cappy flew off the porch, his paws never touching the six steps.

He dashed toward the bull corral, barking his authority. Five, 1,000 pound bulls charged in the direction of the threatening barks. Asserting himself, Cappy belly crawled under the electric fence, hooking his kinked tail around the hot wire at the same time the bulls retaliated with intimidating pawing and beefy bellows.

"Arff, arff, arff, arff!" Cappy cried as he slunk backwards to the safety of the driveway.

"Gotcha, didn't it. Good. Hope you learned a lesson, you stupid city dog."

Equating cattle with painful electric jolts, Cappy learned to focus his energy on stalking ground hogs and raccoons.

Although our rambunctious elkhound never did develop much cow sense, he did watch over our two sons, when he wasn't off on wildlife safaris.

Animal/Feline

Occasionally, ranchers permit an outside cat to become a pampered house pet, particularly when besieged by a nine-year-old child, pleading with his big blue eyes.

"Mommy, pleeese can't we let calico cat come inside? She's so cute," Todd said.

"No. No indoor cats. You can play with them outside. They're much happier hunting and catnapping outside."

"But Explorer..."

"You named a cat? What's wrong with kitty?"

"Explorer is much smarter than the rest of the kittens. I promise I'll never let her into the house when I'm not here."

And so, having a weakness for animals anyway, we gradually allowed this one female cat to worm her way into our house and into our hearts. Explorer found the soft beds—especially our warm waterbed—and followed the warm patches of sunlight streaming through the windows.

At night she continued to hunt rodents outdoors, except when temperatures plummeted fifteen degrees below freezing and Todd, President of the Cat Protection Society, pleaded with us to have compassion for the poor little creature, so defenseless against such extreme weather.

Besides her rodent patrol duties, Ex participated in feline night life, becoming pregnant at predictable intervals. Most of her young joined their cousins in the barn. One summer, however, when both she and two of her last year's kittens all had litters at the same time, I determined to find homes for them. Homes far away from ours.

I delivered one mother and her five nursing kittens to the feed store, four miles from our ranch, feeling relieved I'd found a home with hunting possibilities for all of them.

I would have had the cats fixed, but I was never able to strike a trade with the vet that didn't involve cash. And spending hard earned dollars to spay a female cat was not up for discussion, despite the Cat Society President's able arguments in favor of surgery.

Two weeks after I'd deposited the mousers at the feed store, the proprietor informed me that three of the kittens still roamed his warehouse, but mama cat had disappeared. "Oh," I said, "too bad." I tried to look saddened by this news.

Meanwhile, back at the ranch, I held a kitten-pickin' party. I invited half a dozen victims to our home for dessert one evening, including an unsuspecting minister and his wife and kids. Once there, I explained, as a reward, they were not only among the chosen few who could eat as much lemon meringue pie and jelly rolls as they wanted, but they also had the obligation to pick a kitten to take home with them.

This plan worked only twice. When I attempted a third kitten pickin' party the following spring, I found I had few willing friends left, no matter how tempted they were by my sumptuous desserts.

Compounding the feline overpopulation dilemma, the feed store mama cat returned. Sitting out on the porch one afternoon I noticed a pathetic, scrawny, burr-covered gray cat prowling by the wood pile. Not recognizing her as one of ours, and thinking she must be rabid, I went inside to fetch the .22 rifle.

I returned to see Todd, his blue eyes wide with amazement, sitting on the step with the cat curled tightly on his lap.

"Get away from that thing!" I screamed. "It's probably got rabies or a serious case of worms."

"Mom. This is Ex II. Look at her."

Ex II was on her back purring as Todd stroked her burr-covered belly and told her what a good kitty she was to come home. I put the rifle down and went over to confirm that this unlikely cat was once ours. Sure enough, no mistaking that tiny white spot under the chin.

"Oh, all right, Todd. I guess if the darn cat likes our ranch so badly that she swam rivers, crawled along steep banks, and whatever else she must have gone through to journey back here, she can stay. Are you sure that's the same cat we dropped at the feed store?"

"Yes, Mom."

After Todd fattened her up, I took Explorer and Ex II to the vet's to be spayed. I made Todd promise, right hand held high, that he would never ever bring up the subject with his father. When the bill arrived, I paid it immediately. It never even reached the TO BE PAID pile.

That fall when the vet was out giving vaccination shots to the heifer calves, I asked him to neuter Newt, the male cat. A few swipes with a sharp scalpel, out they came and off Newt ran.

Almost before the wound healed, Newt was killed in a cat fight at the All-Night Cat Cafe. I never again had a male cat fixed.

We enjoyed the antics of our spayed females, who now spent more and more time indoors. Marc assumed old age was the reason there were no more kittens running under foot.

Appliances

Not toasters or roasters

Brand new appliances. That's how much Marc thought of his new bride. Refrigerator. Deep freeze. Washing machine. But, no dryer. There wasn't enough space in the entry/laundry room.

Nor was I jealous of my family and friends who owned dryers. Everyone knows they're hard on clothes. Besides, I would never use one anyway because nothing could match the fresh smell of clothes dried outside in the sun.

For ten years, I dried laundry on a rope strung between a large maple tree and two steel poles. During really bad weather, the wash hung limp on sagging lines of plastic rope secured to the attic walls with fence staples. I trudged up and down two flights of narrow stairs with basket loads of diapers and slow drying blue jeans.

Subconsciously, I thought this arrangement confirmed my pioneering spirit. After all, we didn't own a telephone or a TV set for the first six months of our marriage. We succumbed, at last, to pressure from family and friends to modernize when they tired of us popping over to make phone calls or to watch a "must see" television program. The lack of a dryer, however, didn't inconvenience anyone.

Nor was I discontent when we moved to South Dakota, dryerless. Marc strung up an outside clothesline even before he had fenced off the yard from stray cattle. The clothes dried in less than an hour in this western region of sunny days and low humidity. I even looked forward to the day when I would tell our grandchildren that I had often brought in frozen clothes off the winter line, just as Marc's mother had told our children. Besides, not spending money on electricity for a dryer pleased my thrifty nature.

One summer afternoon, I hung out two loads of wash after lunch, before Marc and I left for a pleasant afternoon irrigating alfalfa and corn fields. That night, after a quick meal of toasted cheese sandwiches, I was too exhausted to bother bringing in the clothes.

When I glanced out our bedroom window the next morning, I saw a naked clothesline. "Jeepers creepers. Someone must be awful desperate to steal clothes off our line!"

I went outside to look but couldn't find even one lone sock. Greatly upset, I walked to the other side of the house to pull sand burr vines from the garden. I noticed what looked like trash blown all over the sage-covered hillside below our house. "Darn wind," I said. "Doesn't it ever quit blowing?"

Wait! That's not trash. It's the laundry! Underwear was festooned and hooked on prickly yucca plants. Work shirts were ripped from blowing across brambly current bushes. And all sizes and colors of socks hid in the tall grass, beside rocks, and in the cedar tree. T-shirts lay in wrinkled heaps, wet with morning dew and covered with earwigs and other nasty night-crawling black bugs. Two loads of wash strewn over a quarter acre beyond the clothesline!

The heck with pioneering spirit. That afternoon Marc and I purchased our first used dryer.

I learned the dryer's rhythm. How to bang the door for a jump start. What the maximum number of loads was before I had to clean the lint filter. And how many minutes of searing heat (the program was simple: One frying hot temperature fits all) a load of delicates could withstand. I liked my dryer.

Blissfully content for six months, I was totally unprepared for a shut down in the middle of a twenty-below-zero spell. I beat the door. I unplugged and plugged in the electric cord. I jiggled the dryer fuse. I whined to Marc.

"Yeah, yeah. I'll take a look at it as soon as I can."

I was patient. I hung wet clothes on the shower curtain rod and laid out underwear on towels covering our bed where morning sunshine streaming through the windows, could dry them.

"And when might that be?" I asked politely, unaware that 'as soon as I can,' really meant 'when I feel like it.'

"I'll look at it tonight after I do evening chores."

"Great."

That night Marc and I assisted a first calf heifer deliver her nine-month burden.

"Tomorrow, after we check the cow herd."

"Great."

Yet another load of clothes hung in the bathroom. "When, dear?"

"Quit harping on me. If you're in such a big hurry, take the wash over to Mom's."

I took the wash to Mom's. Was it my fault I had become dependent on this modern appliance? Mom brewed a cup of hot tea and told me about life in the log house in Canada.

That night I told my honey that I'd called the repairman. Thirty-five dollars for the call, plus milage.

"Are you nuts!" Marc squirmed on the couch, trying to ignore me.

I reminded him the predicted high for tomorrow was ten degrees. "Do you want to hang the clothes outside? Your hands freeze to the cloth. You can barely slap a clothespin on before a shirt is frozen solid. Shucks, I'm lucky if I can jam one clothespin on a pair of underpants before..."

"Nag. Nag. Nag. Turn the TV off and clear the stuff off the top of the dryer. You never give up, do you?"

Marc unfolded his body from the prone couch position and walked to the kitchen. "I don't know anything about dryers and electricity. I hate working with electricity. Scares me to death."

"I know, honey. But I hate to spend fifty bucks to have the

repairman come out if it's something simple."

"So, cancel him. I mean, how difficult can a dryer be?"

"Shall I make you a cup of hot chocolate?"

"A whiskey, maybe. Here, grab hold of the other side. We have to drag the machine out where I can look at it. Why don't those inventor people invent machines with fronts that can be screwed off instead of backs!"

I stood beside my husband, ready to offer encouraging words. How was it he could repair the heater on the stock water tank, but one measly little dryer caused him such aggravation?

He unscrewed the back plate. "The belt's broken."

"Oh," I said. "Is that hard to replace?"

"You didn't tell me there was heat. You said it was broken. If you had said there was heat, but the barrel wasn't moving, I'd have fixed it in a jiff."

This would not be the only appliance war Marc and I would have during our years of wedded bliss. Recognizing how damaging appliance breakdowns were on a marriage, we agreed to spend the big bucks when the washing machine needed replacing.

Our Maytag had a front panel for ease of repair, but even a smoothly-running washing machine can't always prevent arguments over laundry.

In long ago days, I was told, cisterns collected precious rain water. In not so long ago times, when big augers drilled for water, cisterns took on new uses. Ours had been pebbled by shot gun blasts, creating a septic tank for wash water. Deep into the sandy soil the laundry water easily leaked through the bullet holes.

Occasionally, when haying or gardening prevented me from doing wash until we were down to the last pair of underwear, I devoted an entire day to washing our clothes. Sometimes I even threw in curtains and blankets.

This caused the cistern to overflow. The little bullet holes couldn't keep up with the constant supply of water draining into the twenty foot deep corrugated steel tank. No matter. That day the iris under the cottonwood trees got some extra moisture.

During the winter of 1983 the cistern system totally failed.

The temperature in our part of western South Dakota never rose above freezing for two months. The wash water wasn't draining. I threatened to telephone the repair man. I became emotional, spreading my tirades about the house.

"You'd fix this if it had to do with the comfort of a cow. But, no, it's just a household breakdown. A small inconvenience that mere humans should be able to put up with, huh?"

Marc and the boys walked out the back door into the frosty air, preferring to find outside work that required their attention.

"Fine," I hollered out the door. "My clothes will last longer than yours. After you put on the same pair of dirty socks for the third day in a row, maybe you'll take a hint."

Returning to the house much later, at the insistence of hunger pains, Marc was forced to examine the cistern situation.

"Well, Rachel, it's simple. There's not enough drop to the drain hose and when water creeps over the edge of the cistern it immediately freezes. There's not a thing I can do about it. You'll have to wait for a thaw."

"There must be something you can do. Surely the most famous jerry-rigger in the world isn't going to let this simple problem stump him. I know you'll figure out a solution."

I was stymied. Marc had a point, but I didn't like the idea of waiting for a spring thaw. Hauling the wash to town would take forever. I filled the bathtub with hot, sudsy water. As I pressed the dirty shirts into the water, I sang, "This is the way we wash our clothes. Wash our clothes."

I began believing Marc's thaw-solution, when I heard the long range forecast of highs or lows or whatever it is that stalls a freezing front for weeks on end. Wait for a thaw. Life could be so simple for Marc.

At least the dryer worked. I grabbed a basket of hand-washed shirts and dripped my way to the old dryer. I downed a couple of aspirin—my back was killing me—and poured a cup of steaming hot coffee. Sitting by the wood stove, absorbing its luxurious heat, I pondered life, which led me to pondering the frozen drain hose.

"That's it," I said jubilantly. I filled four pans with water and set them to boil on the electric stove. While I waited, the dryer hummed.

I yanked the lose outtake hose from the washer and poured pots full of hot water down the plastic drain pipe. You're such a genius, I told myself. Marc will be amazed when he comes in. I ran outside to see if the blocks of frozen water had slid from the end of the drain pipe. Nothing yet. Another pan of hot water should do it.

"This is the way to fix the pipe. Fix the pipe. Fix the pipe." Down goes the last gallon of hot water, melting, melting. Splash. What's this? Water was overflowing from the inside end of the pipe. Maybe I wasn't so brilliant, after all.

Maybe water had frozen so far up the pipe—fifteen feet or so -that no amount of hot water could break loose the underground frozen water. My husband walked in on my dilemma, put his strong arms around me and whispered, "Spring thaw." I broke down in tears, then sobs, as I considered my great winter of discontent.

The following day, Jerry-rig Marc brought a thirty foot stiff PVC pipe, two inches in diameter. "What's that for?" I asked.

"That, my dear wife, is for the purposes of solving, temporarily, I admit, your washing problem..."

"My washing..."

"Easy. Okay, 'our' washing problem."

Sniffle. Sniffle.

An ice mountain formed where water poured from the end of the temporary pipe. Cold air swept into our warm house while the door was being held open to drain wash water from the temporary pipe. For three months, until the thaw, I babysat clothes washing. Wash. Wash. Hook up the pipe. Run, open the door. Drain. Pull the pipe back in. You get the idea.

Finally, in the first week of May I heard the klunk of melting tubes of ice as they slipped from their long winter's imprisonment. Plunk. Plunk, into the long melted water in the cistern. I doubt there was ever an occasion of more joy or contentment.

Auction

A tractor or a chair

Icy roads, calving cows and haying often prevent ranchers from attending important school board sessions where the fate of our youngsters is decided. But when the auction posters go up in feed stores and banks and ads appear in the Sage News announcing a farm or ranch sale, you can expect to see half the county coming out for this social occasion.

Church auxiliaries and Cattlewomen's organizations vie for the opportunity to increase their coffers by selling home-made pies and sloppy joes. Folks arrive early and stay late.

"Don't worry over Matilda. I checked her before we left. She won't calve until we get home," Marc says with confidence, as we head down the driveway and out to Highway 395 to Gophersburg.

Men inspect the just-have-to-have-tractor-with-front-end-loader-and-less-than-2000-hours-on-it, or a pile of old harnesses that would be nice to fix-up some cold winter day. Women contemplate squandering their $10 on yet another box of old dishes or pots with handles and lids. Nor can we resist the temptation of buying a huge basket of canning jars selling for a buck, even though the canning room is overflowing with empty jars.

At one auction I saw a wife buy a stove for $5. She whispered to the neighbor lady next to her. "That was a great buy. Now I have spare parts for my stove. I've asked George a million times to replace the big front burner. Now, I can do it myself."

Why is one person's junk another's treasure? Why does the farmer, who already has a stack of used tires climbing up the side of his machinery shed, have to buy seven more treadless, wrong size, tires? He argues with his dearly beloved that, "Next year I'm putting up 10 more acres of corn silage. I'll need those extra tires to weight down the tarps."

"Sure," she says and wanders off to look at the bedroom dresser with drawers that slide smoothly in and out.

Potential buyers look over and test the equipment and check through buckets of nails and bolts (the nuts have disappeared).

The first cry from the auctioneer brings spectators front and center with enthusiasm seldom witnessed in a ranching community. I observe a quick exchange between husband and wife as he explains the need to own one more piece of machinery. "Shucks, honey, that junker we have at home's not good for much more than spare parts." Up goes his hand before she can counterattack, the guilt of buying the $5 spare-parts-stove still hanging heavy in the pit of her stomach.

Three hundred gallon fuel tanks are one of the most sought after items at an auction. Competition is always fierce. The new owner of the 6-T ranch property hadn't realized that the fuel tanks didn't come with the place. And war is war. Neighbor against neighbor. Each putting aside their unselfishness as they bid against one another, and the new owner, for possession of a tank. Actually, it's a metal drum so old that moving it from its perch atop the sturdy gasoline soaked wood stand might end its usefulness.

One or two times a year a tractor/machinery dealer decides to sell off inventory. No matter that the sale is 3 hours away. The wife has agreed to stay home and chore. While she prays he listened to her litany-of-the-bills speech, his mind is already figuring out the rationale of why the spreader or rake is the very item he's been searching for—for years.

Auctions bring out the every man/woman for him/her self behavior. I hovered next to a recliner chair, complete with heater and vibrator, waiting for the auctioneer. This wasn't a luxury item. I needed that chair for the next time Marc was down with another one of his back spells. By the time I'd fed out 40 bales of hay in the morning, I was tired. Reclining for an hour after lunch would make it possible for me to get through the afternoon's watering, and chores that evening.

I saw an elderly gentleman meander toward the chair. I quickly rested my hand on the back of the recliner as if to say, "This is mine. Back off. Don't even think of bidding."

I prayed the auctioneer would hurry to the furniture section before others noticed this fine reclining chair. Joe was within two yards of my chair, so I sprawled my arms on top of the chair, in an attempt to lay claim.

The gentleman nonchalantly stopped his meandering within inches of the leather recliner. I stroked the back. Just then the auctioneer and his trailing herd of humanity came upon us.

"Alright, lookee here at this wonderful reclining chair. Rachel, ah, would you step aside so the folks can see this fine leather chair in excellent condition."

Excellent condition. I wished he would use some other adjective to describe my chair. I took a step back.

"Okay, what'll you give me? Twenty-five dollars? Who'll

give me twenty-five dollars?"

I kept my hands tight to my side. I'd been to enough cattle auctions to know you didn't make the first bid.

"Twenty-five from Joe. Thirty. Do I hear thirty? I bet you could sure use a nice lounge chair like this, Joe. Yes, thirty over there. Joe, what'd say, thirty-five? Yes. Now forty. Now forty-five."

Back and forth they went. Come on, I thought, this chair's not worth fifty bucks.

"Back to you, Joe. Will you give me fifty?"

Silence. I shot my hand into the air. Good, the chair was almost mine.

"Well, Mrs. K, where have you been? Okay, fifty from Rachel."

The auctioneer looked toward old man Joe. I glared.

"Fifty-five," says Joe.

"Sixty," says I.

"What do you say, Joe? Gimme sixty-five and the chair is yours."

Wanna bet.

"Sixty-five. Sixty-five. Come on Joe. Take it or leave it. Going once. Going twice. Last chance, Joe. Sold. Rachel, buyer number 18."

I asked Todd to load the chair onto the pickup before I felt too badly about out-bidding old man Joe.

Jim Elliot stood in rapt attention as the auctioneer cried sold. "This fine welder just sold to the gentleman over there." Jim claimed his prize. Then handed his wife a 6 inch stick he had been whittling on. "Here, you hang onto this. If you see me bid on that hay baler, jab me in the ribs with the point of that stick."

Auctions are a form of entertainment for ranchers. For one thing, we don't have to get dressed up. And usually there's free, or at least inexpensive good food available, and, of course, there's all the coffee or Kool-Aid you can drink. Plus, you get to see lots of friends and catch up with all the news and gossip when you're not bidding on that just have to have tractor or reclining chair.

B

Bale

Alfalfa hay bales weigh anywhere from sixty to 135 pounds. Light-weight bales are made by husbands who look at the big picture. Men capable of visualizing their wives lugging hay around while they're at a machinery or cattle auction. Or when they're laid up from back surgery.

Husbands tighten down the bale chambers for medium bales when their only thoughts are strings slipping from loose light bales or small bales that aren't easily picked up by the stacker wagon.

The 135 pounders, usually three wire/twine, are made by people not familiar with the art of physics. Or by twenty-year olds who haven't yet experienced disc surgery. Or by friends who sell the bales to some sucker not smart enough to understand that the stacks of hay dumped on his yard by machine, will be unstacked by hand all winter long in freezing temperatures when a person is so bundled he can barely bend over.

The big round/square bales are the rancher's alternative to crippled backs. Weighing between 650 and 1200 pounds, there's NO WAY to move them by hand. We bought a round baler the spring Marc had disc removal surgery and was laid up for six weeks, all the while listening to me moan, groan, and complain about lugging around heavy, cumbersome hundred pound bales.

I came into the house late after feeding one morning to find Marc, on his back, watching a game show.

"Hey, honey, what took you so long?"

That did it. "You don't know what it's like to be 5' 1-1\2 inches tall and drag a bale around that weighs more than you do. My back hurts. My shoulders ache. I finally cut the strings on the bale and carried the slabs of hay to the trough. How many trips do you think it takes to move one hay bale? And the bulls can just suffer this morning. I didn't have any more energy. I spread the hay out so it looks like they got the full amount."

"Okay. Sorry I asked. Do you want me to come out and help you tomorrow?"

"Oh, sure. And wreck your back all over again. No thanks. Once is enough. How come we aren't modernizing with one of those big round balers?"

"I never thought the little square bales were that much trouble." He stared up at me from his prone couch position, no doubt noticing my diminutive stature. "I suppose maybe we could look into buying a used baler."

"Good idea."

Beer

Summer beverage

Considered a summer beverage, to be consumed at the conclusion of brandings, during dances or at the end of a 14-hour day of hay harvesting. Lowest cost, not fancy title or premium quality, determine the brand.

Bills

So many, so often, so large

Our small ranch is a way station, where the money stops, briefly, before making its way to the deposit window at the big bank in town. Incoming checks for deposit come at infrequent intervals, while the bills arrive constantly and often.

Every month, Marc and I sat at the office desk for our high-pitched, lively discussions on prioritizing the TO BE PAID list. At this time the kids disappeared out the back door.

"Come off it, Marc. We half-paid that dealer off last month. He can wait."

"Yeah, but he's never hassled us. He brings the fuel when we need it. It's not like he has a pile of money..."

"Well..."

"Mark 'paid' by Olly's Oil. We'll see how the rest of the money divies out." Marc then snatched the next invoice off the pile.

Sometimes I considered myself a banker of sorts. During the course of one year, one hundred thousand dollars could easily pass through our checking account. Now, that's a pile of money. But not enough of it stayed in our account.

For example, we sell six bulls. I deposit the check and before it clears, I write out other checks for minerals, electricity, vet, Myron's Mechanics shop and vehicle insurance. If I'm lucky, there's a little left over for groceries and pie and coffee at the cafe.

With hope in our hearts, however, we continue for another month, sure that XYZ Cattle Company will call, looking for that above-average registered bull or a group of line bred Polled Hereford heifers.

On rare occasions when income exceeds outgo and the bill basket is empty—plumb EMPTY—we celebrate with strong drink and dance around the kitchen table.

Birthdays

Bull sales, haying season, county fair

Birthdays are cause for celebration in ranching families. Oh, we work on those special days, too, of course, unless it falls on a Sunday. Then we just work a little less. Unless there is a heifer who needs help calving. Or the hay is dry enough to bale. Or we're halter-breaking bulls for a bull sale. Or it's the day we're vaccinating the cow herd.

But on a day as close to the actual day as possible, we invite family and friends to the ranch, prepare special food the birthday person likes, play cards or horseshoes, or just sit around and shoot the breeze.

Birthdays are an excuse to take a few hours off from our never-ending chores. The size of the gift is less important than the size of the group who gather to sing Happy Birthday. Nor does it matter that little brother iced the cake before it cooled, mixing crumbs with the frosting. And we don't drive twenty miles to town because we forgot to buy candles. We simply recycle the twelve candles saved from the last birthday.

Son Todd celebrated his first three birthdays on March 13, the day on which he was born. For the next fifteen years, though, we celebrated his birthday after our return from a bull sale, before the state breed sale, during the tri-state stock show, but rarely on March 13. When kids asked what day he was born, he said, "Sometime in March."

My husband Marc doesn't care when, or even if, his birthday is celebrated. Psychologists, I'm certain, would conclude that this abnormal behavior is the result of the fact that his special day falls during the time of the county fair. The importance of grooming show cattle overshadows the significance of a mere human's date of birth.

Being an avid birthday person myself, I always tried to work magic on Marc's birthday. One time I got up at five in the morning, whipped up his favorite chocolate cake from scratch and chilled it in the freezer so I could glob the frosting on before we left the house for the fairgrounds.

The weatherman predicted a high of 104 degrees that day, so I packed the cooler with lots of ice and laid the glass baking dish on top. I invited other breeders to join us that evening after the show. Just before we sang our robust version of Happy Birthday, I reached into the cooler to retrieve the cake.

The glass dish and saturated cake had sunk into the melted ice water at the bottom of the cooler. Little bits of chocolate frosting floated to the top. When the laughter died down, we sent five kids off to the dairy booth to buy ice cream cones for everyone.

Given Marc's indifference to making a grand occasion of birthdays, I announced early one June 27th that I planned to take my birthday day off. Period. After Marc and the boys left the house, I grabbed the telephone and invited neighbors and family to join in celebration of my special day at eight o'clock that evening. "No presents, please," I said.

I baked one small fudge cake, an angel food cake and three varieties of pies, including my favorite lemon meringue.

Three hours of uninterrupted scrubbing, dusting and sweeping and the house was immaculate—top to bottom. I spread my grandmother's linen tablecloth over the dining table and set out the array of desserts. I poured a glass of iced tea and lay on the couch to read a book for the remainder of the afternoon.

Fifteen minutes into *Champagne Murders*, however, I grew restless and wondered if I should check on the guys. Nope, I thought—this is my day. If I go out there, they will find something they just absolutely, positively need my assistance with.

Suddenly an idea propelled me off the comfortable couch.

Searching through the house, I located "perfect" gifts I could surprise everyone with that evening. My hunt produced a paperback book, a small plastic ball, unused pens from an insurance company, the bag of M&Ms I'd hidden behind the flour bag, five balls of navy yarn I had bought the previous winter, a Susan B Anthony dollar, a colorful rock and several more items that suited each guest.

I wrote short ditties for each person, which I wrapped with their gift. Later, during coffee and dessert, I handed out these personal thank-yous to the guests, amid much boisterous laughter.

Forgetting Marc's birthday wasn't such a big deal, but, as he likes to tell folks, "Forgetting my wife's birthday, was tantamount to committing the seven deadly sins all at once."

Unfortunately, I was a summer calf. "Oh, I'm sorry I didn't buy you a present," my loving husband told me more than once. "I've been bringing in a year's supply of hay." How could I argue with that?

For years, though, I schemed to bring a measure of importance to my day. I went on cooking strikes, which led Marc to offer me the choice of his taking me out to dinner or him doing the dishes if we ate at home. I still smile when I look at the old framed photo of Marc, bent over the sink, soap suds drifting to his elbows and piles of unwashed pots and pans on the counter.

I tried monthly reminders—starting in February—to increase Marc's awareness of my pending June birthday. "Honey, there are just 127 shopping days left until that magic day in June."

"Oh, okay."

"There are now only sixty shopping days. Maybe next time you're in town, before hay season begins..."

"Yeah, I'll think about it."

He just didn't get it.

Perseverance didn't increase my odds, either, but I never gave up hope. A few years ago, my fortieth birthday dawned warm with bright sunlight and bird songs. As I scooped coffee into the pot I wondered what my husband and teen-aged sons had bought me this year.

Nothing. Not even a birthday kiss or "have a nice day, honey." Not one word of recognition. I sulked. The guys baled hay. I shed a couple of tears. I didn't want them to know how mad and unhappy I was. Fine. They could ignore the most important day of my whole year. I hoed weeds that were overtaking the carrots and spinach. I cursed my inability to make my needs known.

That night, the leftover sunlight and light breeze made perfect baling weather. I soaked in bubble bath, put on a nightgown and climbed into bed. I didn't stir at the sound of the screen door slamming shut. Nor at the whispered conversations.

I was in no mood to be pleasant. I yanked the blanket over my head. My family would never know how upset I was. I feigned sleep when Marc clumped into the bedroom. I was furious when he didn't even lean down to wish me Happy Birthday. Nevermind. I didn't care anymore.

But I suddenly heard footsteps, many footsteps and then, the musical sounds of not one, but many voices singing, "Happy Birthday to you...Happy Birthday to Rachel"...and into our bedroom trooped two dozen family and friends.

"SURPRISE! Thought we forgot, didn't you?" Marc whispered not so quietly. "Get up! Get dressed! It's your birthday!"

I cried.

Budget/Time

Impossible

I've learned over the years that the majority of tasks take longer than expected. If I buy tickets for the Ice Capades—an event that comes to the closest city once every six years—whatever task my husband is doing that day will always take longer than he figured.

If, however, the event is an auction—cattle or machinery— Marc's time budgeting is right on target and at times even early. Odds are that we will arrive long before the auctioneer belts out his first call to action, despite the fact he waited for me to finish 'doing' my hair or drying the one pair of 'good' blue jeans.

We have never worked out an agreeable solution to this, but are now somewhat comfortable in the routine.

"I'm running a little (two hours) late, dear."

"Oh, great. Why didn't you get up two hours earlier, for crying out loud?"

"I can't help it the baler hitch broke."

"So, just leave it till tomorrow."

"And take a chance on rain ruining the hay?"

There was about as much chance it would rain in South Dakota as there was that Marc would be on time, so we accepted these fruitless arguments as a normal part of our life.

Bugs

Annoyances

Generally, those creepy-crawlies that don't sting, suck, or bite are classified under Bug. The larva that infiltrate flour bags or stale cereal, are bugs. They're annoying, but not dangerous or terribly hazardous to our health.

Mosquitos buzzing about my ears after I crawl into bed at night are annoying and they do bite, or is that suck? If they could snack without buzzing, I wouldn't be so frustrated trying to slap them silly. I'd even willingly share my precious blood supply, but the zizzzing and dive bombing makes me snappish and the itching makes me irritable. On the annoyance scale, mosquitoes are right up there with icky brown moths.

They crawl into and out of every nook and cranny in the house. You open the curtains in the morning and a troop of them fly from their resting spots. Though noiseless, they hover and fly slowly around the living room, as if they know this tics us off.

My mother, visiting once from Florida actually threatened to leave, if Marc and I didn't do something about the disgusting brown moths.

One night I walked from our bathroom to the sound of banging doors. "What are you doing?" I asked Mother. She was swishing the air with the livestock newspaper.

"Turn on the other lamp in the living room, Rachel. I'm making a light trail to the front door for the moths. I've swished them from Darryl and Todd's room and my room."

She took more swipes down the hallway, turning lights off along the path of her paper chase. And sure enough a herd of brown moths soon gathered in the living room.

"That's right. Now turn that far lamp off. I've turned the outside light on. Grab the want ads section and drive those little buggers towards me. I'll open the door just as you turn off the green lamp."

I barely escaped with my arm as Mother slammed the door shut. We peeked through the window at the swarm of moths fighting for a place next to the heat of the front door light bulb.

"There, you see Rachel, if we make a sweep every night before we go to bed, we can sleep in peace."

Mom and I continued the moth patrol every evening, ridding the house of hundreds of those pesky, dusty annoying moths. The night after Mom left, I approached Marc about replacing her on the moth swat team.

"What moths?" he said.

Bull

Testosterosis-pain-in-the-neckus

The male of the species displays behavior known as testosterosis-pain-in-the-neckus. Bull animals break out of any enclosure—barbed wire, pig panels, board rail, or electric fence (though admittedly, breakouts from hot wire enclosures only occur when ranchers forget to plug the electricity back in, or when fierce wind storms hurl large limbs upon the fence, grounding the wires) to soothe their restless male urgings.

Bulls express their clout either with the mature composure of a lover bull or with the strident behavior of a fighter.

Upon sensing a neighbor bull prowling toward the common fenceline, lover bulls herd their allotted females to the far corner of the pasture. Lover bulls maintain order much like a stud horse, circling to contain possible curiosity seekers who attempt to wander over to inspect the neighbor bull.

Some bulls merely bellow warnings of superiority. And then there are the newly initiated into the kingdom-of-maleness-bulls, the fighters, who sense competition and leap into action, rubbing the fence until staples fly and entry is gained into the opposing bull's domain.

Older bulls dominate yearling bulls, through roaring and physical combat, signaling that they're not yet ready to share their kingdom of service. Several rough blows to the abdomen convince the younger bulls to remain on the outskirts, close enough to see and smell the action, but far enough away so as not to become injured.

Trial and error teaches the newly initiated that when there is above-average activity, they can slip into the fray as exhaustion overtakes their superiors. If they don't dally they may even breed one

of the many cows, before slipping again to the sidelines.

Testosterosis-pain-in-the-neckus can cause pain in other body parts as well. Physical feats of dominance by large bulls can result in broken legs, severe back strains, pulled stifle muscles, and the breaking or injury of parts required if the animal is to successfully complete his mission in life.

When injury necessitates the removal of an older bull from the breeding pasture, a younger bull is ready to assume his duties, including the physical feats of dominance, which perpetuates not only the species, but also the syndrome of testosterosis-pain-in-the-neckus.

Bulling

Restless urgings

Bulling is the behavior exhibited by cows whose estrus cycle prompts them to seek out a bull. They stand at attention as another female jumps them from behind, creating a scene soon to be investigated by a bull. Normally cows are content with the services of the sire provided for them. On occasion, however, when he doesn't meet her expectations, she wanders over to the fence to hum her tune to the neighbor's bull. Rarely, however, does she make the leap of faith into his pasture. Her goal is to tempt the neighbor bull into joining her on her side of the fence.

She merely waits as neighbor bull gallops over to check out the fence cow. Sensing this to be a good match, neighbor bull continues his stand, nosing through the barbed wire or reaching his head over the top of the fence. If neighbor bull is well-behaved, or remembers his last encounter with his opposition, he stays put. The cow, unsatisfied, heads back to her herd, leaving neighbor bull bellowing and pawing until he gives up and ambles back to his own harem.

Unless, of course, neighbor bull is a fighter and feels compelled to join the female in her pasture. This insures another bout of testosterosis-pain-in-the-neckus.

C

Calves

Personality plus

Calves, like the young of many species, are cute, rambunctious, curious, playful, and dependent on their mothers. Tourists driving by a pasture may assume that a calf is a calf is a calf, but ranchers know that calves have individual personalities.

Paranoid Trash Can Annie, the gentlest of the calves we showed at county and state fairs, once went berserk in the show ring. As I led her around the ring, she spied a styrofoam cup on the ground close to the grandstand. She panicked, jumped into the air, dodged sideways, and ran off, dragging the leather lead strap, leaving me to look like a fool.

A line of spectators and exhibitors captured her and handed the lead strap back to me. She looked at me as we began our march around the ring again. At the paper cup site I also saw a fifty-five gallon trash barrel, and not certain which item had spooked her, I led her toward the inside of the show ring. But it was too late. She went nuts, and I tried hanging onto the leather halter. The judge suggested I lead her to the far end of the arena and stand there.

Because we had never worked with such a quiet calf that suddenly developed paranoia, Marc and I decided that was an isolated incident. With no qualms we kept her in the state fair show string. But when Marc led her into the barn, suddenly the darting, twisting, leaping action began. Sure enough, there was a trash can in the alley next to our tie-in spaces. Now Marc hung on for dear life, while I rolled the can out of sight. With the trash can gone, the calf placidly stepped up to the fence and helped herself to a large serving of sweet-smelling alfalfa hay.

I looked around. There were trash cans everywhere. I'd never seen so many. We couldn't possibly lead her to the outdoor show ring without sighting one of those big ugly monsters. Trash Can Annie remained tied the remainder of the fair!

Performer calves, males and females alike, are the show-offs. The extroverts. They practice leaps, back leg kicks, 100-yard dashes, all with head held high, as they command the attention of their peers. I witnessed a performer jumping into the air, all fours off the ground, only to land flat onto his side. Not the least bit humiliated, he clambered up, dashed off a few yards and ended his routine with the bucking bronc back leg thrust.

Show-off calves crave attention. I've watched a high energy performer charge into a group of laid back sleepers, let out a come-to-attention calf bawl, and once all eyes were on her, dance her jig. Three-quarter turns. Stop on a dime, four feet perfectly placed. Her tail moving rhythmically keeping time to her inner tune.

Pokey calves never hurry anywhere. They seem among the more curious. They investigate all aspects of their world. They sniff down gofer holes. They stand still at the sight of a slithering snake, watching and waiting until the wriggly reptile moves away.

The curious Pokey calves, rather than taking part, are content to stare at the action. An eagle swoops to retrieve a kangaroo mouse lunch while Pokies watch at close range. They remain content as they stand quietly on the outskirts of the calf play area, observing the calf version of King Of The Manure Pile.

They are troublesome when we move cattle, as they continually lag behind, stopping along the way to taste test weeds or poke their heads under the barbed wire fence to explore speedy pheasant chicks .

Pokey calves grow up satisfied with the routine of their lives. Often it is the once pokey heifer calf who, upon reaching motherhood becomes the calm baby-sitter, watching over her charges while the other mothers are off grazing in the distance.

Playful calves exude joy in all their activities. They wag their tails faster while nursing. They nod their heads back and forth as they cavort about the pasture. These fun-loving calves, I swear, have a sense of humor.

My father-in-law and I had to treat a playful calf who, even in sickness, never lost her exuberance. I straddled the calf to hold her steady while Dad slipped the tube down her throat to administer the bag of liquid medication. I held the bag high while he maneuvered the tube into place and opened the snap that allowed the liquid to flow through to her stomach.

Half the contents had drained into the heifer when, suddenly, she erupted with the gentlest of bucks, causing my feet to leave the ground. She began crow hopping and bucking in a straight line, with me still astride holding the bag high, the end now dangling along the ground. I tried dismounting from the 200 pounds of bucking heifer to the sound of Dad's booming laughter. The sight of my hilarious predicament immobilized him. I was finally able to leap ungracefully to the ground. The heifer stopped immediately and looked at me. I could swear her eyes were twinkling.

Pesty calves, often the ones who have bonded with humans during the calving and subsequent nursing lessons, are forever confused as to their species identity.

Pesty calves seek us out, following close by while we cut the twine on hay bales. Eager for a scratch behind the ear or on the

throat, they ignore their natural instincts, approaching their human playmates from ail sides.

One Pesty calf sidled up against my leg for a calming rub. Then she initiated the touch and run game, first standing close for a scratch on the head, then running off in mock fear. She immediately repeated the game, of course, as often as I'd play with her.

Pesty calves also study human behavior. Once, while I was bent over cutting twine, a pesty calf rear-ended me with his head, causing me to lose my balance and flop onto the bale. "Get away from me, you rascal!" I shouted. He walked to the end of the uncut bales and waited patiently while I carried on with my twine-cutting tasks. Ten minutes later a surprise attack from the rear knocked me over again. Pesty stared at me with an "I gotcha" look and put his head down for the expected scratch.

Pitiful Pansies resemble the whiners of the world. Malcontents and martyrs from birth, nothing pleases them. Though they are aggressive nursers, butting their mothers unmercifully, they don't venture far from their protection. When called to come out and play with their siblings, they go forth timidly, usually lose the King Of The Manure Pile game, and quickly return to their mother's side.

Pitiful Pansies prefer isolation to the competitive spirit of the calf pack. They linger on the outskirts longing to join in, but unable to get up enough gumption to charge into the confusing fray.

Pitiful Pansies recover slowly from illness. When a playful or pesty or even the paranoid calf is medicated for scours, for instance, one or two treatments is generally sufficient. But the Pitifuls require four or five treatments. Of course, the longer recuperation period magnifies their already sorry disposition which compounds their pitiful lives. Oh, woe is me, seems their lot in life.

But we ranchers look forward to calving season because the new calves are evidence of last year's optimistic breeding decisions. We linger in the calving pasture to watch the play yard of personalities. The happy-go-lucky and the aggressors. The know-it-alls, as well as the whiners and the sweet tempered. The ornery and the shy calves. While they entertain each other, we look on and enjoy being spectators for awhile.

Cattlemen/Cattlewomen/Cattlechildren

Why'd you let that calf sneak past?

Ranchers—men, women and children alike—are addicted to livestock in general and cattle in particular. Granted, there are days when the stack of bills is too high, or the well engine quits, or the snow is three feet deep, that ranchers consider other means of employment, but mostly there are days when no other occupation satisfies us the way taking care of cattle does.

On the days when taking care of cattle involves branding, herd health, pregnancy testing, or sorting cattle into breeding pastures, teamwork is vital. One time when Marc and I traded cattle work with our neighbors, Chuck and Tammy, things got a little tense.

"Rachel, anticipate. Anticipate," Marc yelled from behind a cow. "It's going to take us till tomorrow if you keep letting the cows burst through the head gate before they've had their shots."

"Oh, shut up, Marc. If you wouldn't 'spook' them into the squeeze chute, I'd have a crack at catching them."

So, we split the couples to create a more harmonious and effective work team. If Chuck was pushing cattle through the chutes, I managed the head catch. When Marc was at the back end shoving the animals through, Tammy took charge of head catching. We noticed that the mixed team approach worked well. We yelled at the animals rather than at our mates.

For the most part working cattle in the chutes became routine, except when an animal behaved unpredictably like the time Tammy was in the alleyway holding back the next group of black baldies ready to come through the chute. Suddenly, one outraged cow took a dislike to her and charged. Tammy screamed, "Chuck, help!"

As Tammy propelled her short, stubby legs down twenty yards of alleyway, the cow breathing down her backside, not one man jumped in to turn the cow back or close a gate. No, they were laughing their fool heads off at the sight of Tammy maintaining her slight lead in front of the snorty four-legged cow.

Tammy hurdled the Power River panel at the end of the chute like she was in training for the Olympics, her feet barely touching the bars as she sailed over to safety. The cow nearly knocked herself silly when she crashed into the gate, just seconds later.

Still choking with laughter, Chuck sauntered over to his wife. "Woman, a few more yards and you would have been flying without wings."

"I wish you could have seen yourself," Marc offered. "Could we see that again, Tammy, in slow motion?" Marc broke up laughing.

"Hush up, Marc," I said. "Tammy was nearly mowed over by that mean cow."

Tammy, winded from her twenty yard dash, picked up a sorting stick and approached Chuck. "DON'T ever call me woman again!" She paused to catch her breath. No one was laughing now. Not even a cow sound broke the silence. Bringing the stick back, ready to swing, Tammy stopped just as Chuck stepped to the side. "I was nearly killed back there. I would have died to the sounds of your laughter, and you would have felt guilty for the rest of your life." She tossed the stick over by the chute. "I was pretty darn fast, wasn't I?"

When Marc and I worked our cow herd by ourselves, we had a pretty good system. If Marc got too out of sorts when I didn't hurl myself in front of an escaping 1200-pound cow, I reminded him that cheap help had the option of leaving the scene and returning to the house. My skill levels increased in direct proportion to the increase in Marc's patience. We developed a system of directional hand signals and complex voice commands such as "yo" or "watch it" which we used in combination to maintain order.

When school let out for the summer, our sons joined us in the corrals to help ear tag eighty-five calves. Unfortunately, the harmony that existed when Marc and I worked the animals, evaporated once our team expanded to four. The inbred pecking order took over. Marc hollered at me, I hollered at the boys, and oldest brother picked on youngest brother. The cows, of course, took complete advantage of the confusion and havoc resulted. The animals mixed easily between sorting pens, charged through the head catch without being caught and tried jumping out of the chute. As emotional leader, I called a ten-minute organizational recess.

"No, let's keep going," Marc said, apparently oblivious to

how confused the situation had become, "I want to finish up before lunch."

"Before lunch! The way we're going, we'll be lucky if we sit down to supper by seven o'clock."

"Yeah, Dad. It's your fault Bossy snuck through to the other pen. If you..."

"Yo. Stop right there, Darryl. Now, listen up, everyone." I paused while the animals mooed in a loud chorus. "Here's my idea. I think we agree that the faster we get done, the sooner we can eat. We know that the cattle are already stirred up, so, how about if we make corral work a special day. Anyone can say anything they want to the cows, to their brother, their husband, wife or parent..."

"Alright," Todd chimed in, "this is going to be fun. Hey, Mom, pretty stupid of you to let that last cow bully her way by you!"

"Oh, and you would have been able to stop her." I shot back.

"You have to anticipate," Marc said. "And be quicker. This is the slowest bunch of cow punchers I've ever worked with."

"Okay, the deal is, when we're through the work, we wipe the slate clean, blame our anger on the cows, and head to the house as friends.

Three heads nodded agreement. We settled down. The cattle settled down. And we were in the house for lunch by 1:30.

A different style of teamwork is required when ranchers work large numbers of cattle. In this case there are a number of unwritten laws about the division of labor. Men shall sit atop mighty steeds to rope calves. Men shall castrate bull calves. Men shall press the red hot branding iron to the calf's hide. Women shall fill vaccine guns, wrestle calves to the ground, do the paperwork and operate the head catch. Children shall assist where needed, be it fetching jugs of iced tea or keeping hungry calves from returning to their mothers.

Cattlemen separate the cattle. Catlewomen and cattlechildren work the gates and are chewed out by cattlemen when a calf sneaks through.

Cattlewomen are the persons who begin work at 4:30 in the morning preparing food AND working cattle AND at noon finishing the preparation and serving food to cattlemen who are sprawled under shade trees, resting from their hard labors. Alright, cattlemen and cattlechildren usually get up early too, to round up the critters.

Depending on the availability of help on branding day, some of the tasks fall into neutral territory where either gender may sort cattle, push cattle through the chutes, operate vaccine guns, or clamp in ear tags, without giving up their identity.

Roping calves, though, is strictly in the male domain of job descriptions. Except at Tammy and Chuck's ranch at branding time. Their five children had been riding horses soon after they were potty trained. Donna, the oldest child, had been roping kid sisters and brothers, fence posts, hay bales, sheep — when her mom wasn't looking — and quiet 4-H steers, since she was a little shaver.

Two years into her teens, Donna declared that this year, "I'm gonna rope calves, Mom, not wrestle them." She sat short in the saddle on top her sorrel gelding, amongst the older experienced men, quietly operating her lariat as rhythmically as her sister fingered the keys on the family's upright piano.

Loop after loop, Donna would catch the back legs of the calves milling in the catch pen and then calmly pull them to the wrestlers. Big George, considered to be one of the finest ropers in the county, stared at this little gal as though she were intruding on men's work. Undaunted, Donna continued throwing her perfectly-timed loops, making catch after catch.

I watched her dad give her the thumbs up sign when she hit the mark and Big George was gathering in his second empty rope. At noon, Donna unsaddled her horse and went inside to help the ladies prepare dinner.

While all of us were eating on the shaded front lawn, I saw Big George walk over to Donna. "You're pretty good with that lariat, young lady." Then he tipped his cowboy hat and wandered off to where the guys were swapping ranching war stories.

At the end of the long taking-care-of-cattle-days, the youngsters leaped onto their steeds and drove the cattle out to pasture while the adults, males and females together, sipped summer beverages and told tall tales.

Characters

People aren't always what they seem

"What was that?" Marc yelled over the engine noise as our 1956 stake bodied Chevy truck climbed a hill fifty miles west of Pittsburgh.

Though his foot was on the gas pedal, the speedometer needle was dropping. We heard no evil grinding noises, but we felt a pulling against the forward movement.

"We're not out of gas, are we?" I asked guardedly. Hitchhiking to a gas station, however, seemed like a pleasant activity, compared to a major engine failure at 1 a.m.

The truck quit before Marc was able to steer it to the shoulder of the highway.

"Moooo. Mooooo...moo...moo."

"Oh, great, the bull's nervous. He's shaking the truck. Keep your foot on the brake," I yelled, "until I shove the block behind the tire."

"Damn hand brakes," said Marc. "You jump up here and hold the break pedal down. I don't trust that block to hold on this steep incline."

"Moo...Moo..."

"Easy, boy," I called out the window.

Not finding an obvious mechanical problem under the hood, Marc shined the flashlight under the truck. "Beats me," he said. He walked to the back to check the wood block holding the two-ton vehicle and swaying one-ton bull.

"Oh, boy!"

I felt the back tire rocking on the block and jammed my shaking foot harder against the brake pedal. "What? What's wrong?"

"We're frozen up."

"CAN YOU FIX IT?"

"Come here, Rachel, and look at this. NO, forget that, just stay where you are and keep pressure on the brake!"

He walked to the driver's window and peered in at me. "It's

bad. Looks like the wheel froze to the spindle. We're going to need a tow."

The quiet night surrounded us. I had to pee. Marc leaned against the truck.

The restless bull mooed and paced.

Within minutes, we saw flashing lights. "What's the problem?" the state trooper hollered. The bull reached his head over the side and pawed the boards, and let out his own rank bellowing.

Marc flashed the light on the wheel and axle.

"Look's like you're stuck." The officer touched the axle. "Whew. That's one hot puppy. Well, I'm not sure what can be done on a Sunday. I'll call Jimmy up for a tow." He sauntered off to his patrol car.

Marc pulled out his wallet. "Fifty-five bucks. Now's when I wish we had a credit card."

"I woke Jimmy up. He was kind of grumpy, but he'll come get you as soon as he downs some coffee. It's only about ten miles into town." He drove off into the night.

"This is going to cost a bundle, huh?" I leaned against the door.

"Good thing the cattle sold well. Dang it! I wish we hadn't volunteered to haul this bull." Marc frowned and tried to soothe the frightened animal.

Forty-five minutes later good old Jimmy showed up. After surveying the situation he said, "Damn, this is going to be tough, folks, with that one-ton chunk of beef in the back."

Maybe the dark surroundings and bleak outlook of our circumstances influenced my level of fear, but Jimmy was the scariest, most ominous looking person I had ever seen in my entire twenty-eight years. All three hundred burly, bearded pounds of him. It seemed as though dark, scraggly hair grew in masses everywhere on his body. His narrow eyes, his sullen attitude didn't inspire a whole lot of confidence. Actually, I was scared to death. I whispered to Marc that I wouldn't mind spending the rest of the night in the truck. We could call for help again during daylight hours. I imagined all sorts of horrors.

Was The Bearded One an evil drug dealer? Was he in cahoots with the state trooper? Cop locates stranded motorist and good old Jimmy hauls them to his wrecking yard filled with vehicles taken because the innocent traveler can't produce enough cash to pay off the exorbitant towing and repair bill?

My fear increased in direct proportion to my need to find a restroom. My bladder was ready to pop. I had switched feet several times on the brake as each leg turned numb. What was I going to say, "Excuse me, most huge sir, would you hurry up and hook our truck to yours. I really have to go badly?" I tried to control my bladder and thought about why we were so determined to drive all the way home right after the sale. We could have been sound asleep in a nice motel in Zanesville, Ohio. But no, we HAD to get home. Cows calving. Hay to sell.

Marc and Jimmy finally managed to secure our crippled vehicle to the tow truck and off we drove at twenty-five miles an hour. I kept my eyes glued on the bull so I could report any wild leaping activity. I prayed Marc was keeping a close eye on our three hundred pound driver.

We pulled into Jimmy's wrecking yard at about 3:30 a.m. "Let's go to the house," Jimmy said and led the way. I followed close behind. At this point I didn't care if he planned to tie us up and shoot our bull. I could concentrate on one thing only—finding a bathroom.

Jimmy's wife was lounging at the kitchen table. I looked at her. She was gorgeous. I felt like a truant teenager. "Ma'am," I asked, "may I use your bathroom?"

"Sure, honey. First door on your right, down the hall."

Returning to the kitchen, I was relieved to see that Marc wasn't tied up. A half smile creased Jimmy's face above the bushy beard, and his gorgeous wife was pouring four mugs of freshly brewed coffee. The atmosphere wasn't fearful at all, it was warm and friendly. My impending scenario of doom evaporated on the spot.

Marc had telephoned my brother, who lived in Pittsburgh, an hour's drive from Jimmy's place. He was on his way to pick us up. Jimmy assured Marc there was a used axle on an old school bus back of his garage and that he could install it in the morning. And Jenny, his charming wife, served warm cinnamon buns and refilled our coffee.

The four of us chatted like old friends about the Pirates pennant chances that year. I figured anyone who enjoyed baseball couldn't be all bad. I watched Jimmy tip his chair back on two legs, and rest his hairy arms to the side. There was no weapon under his vest.

"Are you okay?" Jenny asked. "You look a mite trembly."

"Yes, thank you, I'm fine. Real good. Must be all the excitement tonight."

"Well, listen, honey, don't you worry about a thing. My Jimmy's the best mechanic around. He'll get your truck running, won't you Jimmy-Jim?"

"Yep. As long as that axle fits, it won't be no problem. And don't you worry none about the bull. I'll drive the whole shebang into the garage. Leave the lights on. I think he'll be okay, don't you, Marc?"

My brother drove us back to Jimmy's in the morning and we were on our way again by noon. The bull had weathered the experience just fine. Jimmy wouldn't let Marc pay for anything. "Hey, buddy, the next time you see someone in trouble, give him a hand, okay, and we'll call it square."

On Monday, I mailed a thank you letter and a check to cover towing, parts, a few hours labor and an extra twenty for kindness shown to us by this most fearsome good samaritan and his gracious wife.

Church of Agriculture

Thou shalts

The Church of Agriculture owns no buildings. Holds no services. Yet, it ministers to every man, woman and child earning their livelihood from the land.

The evolving dogma, refined through generations of pragmatic testing, dictates a rancher's behavior, binding him and her to its credos in a culture where individualism is worshipped and admired, but only when it works for the well being of all.

Following is a list of some of the more common commandments. Should a member of the Church of Agriculture fail to adhere to any one of these rules, he or she will suffer a variety of consequences, not the least of which is ostracization from the culture of ranching and farming. Membership is not optional.

• *Thou shalt not own late-calving cows.*

In particular, the *last* cow to calve. Better that she be shipped to the butcher than allow her a repeat performance.

• *Thou shalt not call a vet...*

... until you've exhausted all other possibilities for doctoring a sick critter. All other includes using every bucket, hose, pill and liquids (medication, water, mineral oil, Kaopectate, Pepto Bismal). It also includes calling neighbors for help, both physically and emotionally, for their advice on how they've solved the problem in the past.

Being constantly short on cash motivates cattlemen to adhere to this law. Consequences of delaying a visit to a vet may, however, cause greater draining of financial reserves. This is usually due to an animal's severely weakened condition once the decision is finally made to summon a veterinarian's expert assistance.

• *Thou shalt be the first in your county to swath hay.*

The implied significance being that you were also the first to oil, grease, sharpen and repair the equipment in preparation for haying season. And this also implies that you drove the cattle off the fields early enough to create an environment wherein rain and warm temperatures could start the growing cycle.

• *Thou shalt not be guilty of moving hay stacks early to winter feeding area—usually near house and corrals.*

The consequences of ignoring this rule may result in pre-winter thunder storms where lighting seeks out large early-moved hay stacks, placed next to each other, as an easy target for total destruction of an entire winter's feed supply, as well as the threat to owner's house.

• *Thou shalt not be the last to plant corn.*

Unless you're borrowing the neighbor's planter and he chooses to sow his fields first and yours last.

The consequences of failure to plant crops early, regardless of the variety, include, but are not limited to (1) embarrassment (2) harassment by earlier planting neighbors who may laugh derisively and gloat unnecessarily and (3) strong possibility that the first frost may occur prior to the completion of the kernel maturation process.

• *Thou shalt not own less land than your neighbor.*

This leads to obvious complications of price inflation due to land grabbing and can cause an inability to manage mortgage payments.

• *Thou shalt be grateful for 115 degree heat.*

The alternative is -30 degree cold.

• *Thou shalt be grateful for -30 degree cold.*

Remember the 115 degrees in the shade last summer?

• *Thou shalt not complain during blizzards,*
where three feet of wet snow accumulates.

The occurrence of any moisture is to be applauded.

• *Thou shalt be grateful for any type of moisture.*

Be it drifts of snow, regular slow descending rain, rain that causes flood conditions, rain that creates gumbo glue, or the moisture that comes from hail. Well, okay, not hail. The destructive capabilities of hail outweigh the moisture benefits.

• *Thou shalt be permitted to comment on constant 50 mph winds,*
regardless of the season.

Excessive cursing, however, is not permitted.

• *Thou shalt tolerate with minimum complaining.*

Stinging bees, biting ants, welt-producing heal flies, or noisy, blood sucking mosquitos. They must be considered part of the price of doing business in the country and fall into the If-you-want-this-you-must-put-up-with-that syndrome.

• *Thou shalt help thy neighbor in a crisis.*

During storms of all kinds—snow, dust, fire.

When the neighbor requests help with calving difficulties.

When the neighbor is laid up from back surgery or recuperating from a fall off a frightened horse. The rancher shall do chores, put up hay or harvest the crop that was ready just before the neighbor was sidelined.

• *Thou shalt assist neighbors even when not in crisis.*

With cattle work, particularly at branding time, but also at vaccination and herd health time and at round-up time, both for gathering cattle from pastures and for sorting, once the bovines are corralled. Additionally, as a good-standing member of The Church of Agriculture, ranchers agree to assist with hollering, yelling and coaxing animals into livestock trailers.

A rancher may send out an SOS when animals stray outside the owner's boundaries and extra bodies are needed for gate-watchers, section-line watchers, or when cattle on roads and highways require traffic directors.

When absolutely unavoidable, ranchers shall help neighbors

who raise hogs, especially when they're bartering cattle work or machinery work for hog moving or hog chores while swine owner attends state fair.

Assisting a neighbor may also require a cattleman, understandably under duress, to work with sheep, but only in the case where one's sheep neighbor also runs cattle. And, then, neighbor should only call when he is in dire need of services for help with loading sheep into tractor trailers that are heading to the market.

• *Thou shalt experience awe and appreciation for...*

The birth of each live, healthy calf.

For a dark night sky so filled with star constellations that everyone stands in silence.

For rainbows across an expansive sky, even when no pots of gold are discovered.

For sunrises, though not as deeply moving as the purples and reds of sunsets, still they brighten and bring warmth to the lives of beasts and mankind alike.

For the quiet prairie splendor and its inhabitants, both animal and vegetable.

For the steadfastness of families and friends who share both joys and sadnesses.

• *And lastly, thou shalt strive...*

To become a knowledgeable steward of the land on which we all reside for such brief moments. A land that we bequeath to future generations, hopefully, in better condition than when we arrived. Harmony and balance. Order and peace. Yes, even when life seems the most unbalanced and chaotic.

Cooking

Mama mia

When I began married life with a rancher—before becoming one myself—I thought it was enough that I loved the animals. And that I didn't mind spending an afternoon helping Marc string barbed wire, instead of mall shopping. That I preferred the outside chores to the inside chores.

Inside chores included cooking, an art I had little experience with. I enjoyed eating my mother-in-law's fried chicken, zesty meat loafs and every baked item in her yeasty repertoire. I didn't understand the mysteries of cooking, nor had I thought much about my husband's love of hearty meals. Cooking and food wasn't a top item in our premarriage discussions. Do you suppose this man thought ALL women knew their way around the kitchen?

Not only had Marc purchased a spanking new 20 cubic foot chest freezer just prior to our marriage, he filled it with beef. Cuts of beef with names I didn't recognize. New York steak. Rump roast. Heart. Short ribs. Nor were there recipes on the white wrapping that suggested how I might cook these strange cuts of meat.

I did catch on quickly that the Noon Meal was the BIG meal of the day. And so it was, in the era before microwaves, the pressure cooker became my friend. One morning, a week after we returned from our honeymoon, I awoke inspired to prepare a hearty meal using the short ribs.

While the package thawed, I consulted my Betty Crocker Beginner Cookbook. No short ribs recipe. By ten o'clock that morning I panicked. Marc would be in for the Noon Meal in two hours and I hadn't the foggiest notion how to cook partially frozen short ribs. Nor had I thought to thaw a package of ground beef as a back up.

Angry at our decision not to install a telephone (didn't want our newly wed privacy interrupted), I ran the quarter of a mile to my sister-in-law's house for her advice. Suzanna was an excellent cook. She even maintained her composure, keeping her giggles under control, while I blithered my dilemma.

Being a woman of great resource, Suzanna offered two options. 1. "Why don't you and Marc eat lunch with us? I have a roast in the oven. We'll just peel a couple more potatoes and Marc will never know about your, giggle, giggle, dilemma." Or 2. "You can run home, 'thaw' the short ribs in the pressure cooker for about ten minutes and arrange them on a cookie sheet. Spread a sauce made of ketchup, two teaspoons of vinegar, and a 1/2 cup brown sugar, over top and pop them in the oven for an hour and a half at 350 degrees. Boil potatoes and a vegetable and you're a star."

"Suzanna, you're an angel!"

I hugged my sister-in-law and dashed home to put option two into action. Because we had eaten a lot of meals with Suzanna and John, I secretly feared eating one more of her great meals might cause Marc to suspect my cooking abilities.

The baking short ribs, smothered in brown sugar and ketchup, smelled wonderful. I whipped the potatoes extra long so they were smooth like my mother-in-law's. And I cooked lima beans, Marc's favorite vegetable. My ploy worked. My new husband dug in as though he hadn't eaten in twenty-four hours. The fact that he didn't slap me on the back and say, "Great meal," meant that the Noon Meal went off normally.

By haying season I had gained much more confidence in my ability to put a meal on the table. I also called the telephone company to bring a phone line to our house. Running back and forth from Suzanna's was too time consuming. I needed telephone service for emergency advice.

Day after day the guys stacked wagon loads of hay into cavernous barns. Because several of the fields were miles away from the home place and also because rain clouds threatened to dampen the work, Marc asked me to bring the Noon Meal out to the fields in order to save time.

We ranch wives alternated cooking the Noon Meals. The cold roast beef sandwiches and watermelon slices brought no complaints. My confidence continued to increase and the worry lines eased from my brow.

I decided I was ready for the challenge of preparing the full meal deal. The day before, I set two packages of hamburger in the refrigerator to thaw. No last minute pressure cooking. Then, in the morning, shortly after Marc and the crew left on tractors for the southeast field I set out jugs of sun tea and refilled the ice trays.

The excitement of surprising the men with a non-sandwich meal filled me with the desire to become the best cook ever. "Cooking is fun," I said aloud as I browned the ground beef. I added canned tomatoes, tomato paste, onions, and the spices listed in the spaghetti sauce recipe.

The aroma rising from the simmering sauce filled the kitchen. With each stir I felt the pride and joy of doing a job and doing it well. I made just one emergency phone call to Suzanna during the morning's food preparation. "Hey, Suz, how often do you stir the sauce?"

Keeping in mind the fifteen minute drive out to the field, I set a large soup kettle on the stove to boil water for spaghetti noodles.

The sauce simmered. The spaghetti bubbled. I packed the picnic basket with plates, silverware, napkins, parmesan cheese, rolls and butter and plastic glasses. I set the two gallon jugs of iced tea on the floor of the driver's side of the pickup where I could steady them as I drove over the bumpy dirt road. I began to perspire from the ninety-four degree heat. I imagined how much the crew would appreciate the iced tea.

With joy in my heart I smiled at the thought of how pleased Marc would be with his city wife. Reaching the field I heard the tractors at the far end, and quickly, I spread out the food in the shade of the tree row.

The guys turned the engines off and I ran to greet my husband. He gave me a squeeze and said, "What's for Noon Meal? We're starved."

I proudly lifted the lids on my morning's labor. Marc looked at the simmering sauce.

"Spaghetti!" he howled. "You fixed spaghetti on the hottest day of the year? We're sweating like pigs already and you're feeding us hot spaghetti with spicy sauce?" He looked at my crestfallen face,

then at the crew. "Well, come on, guys," he said, "we better eat some of this."

Barely able to hold back my tears, I dished out the hot, spicy spaghetti. I was thankful they were in a hurry. Within twenty minutes they had wolfed down the hot stuff and were up and heading back to the equipment. As I began to pack up my disastrous full meal deal, tears cascaded down my dusty cheeks and great sobs overtook me. I hadn't noticed Marc climbing down from the tractor until I felt his arm around my shoulders.

"I'm sorry, honey. I didn't mean to hurt your feelings. Sandwiches are fine on a day like this. Maybe you can freeze the rest of the spaghetti?" He patted me on the rump and hustled back to the tractor.

I wiped the tears with my T-shirt. I'll ask my Suzanna about freezing. She'll know what to do.

Cooking/Recipes

Glass baking dishes

Whether at home or carried to pot lucks at brandings, to birthday celebrations, to 4-H functions, or to county fairs, ranch wives would be seriously incapacitated without several 9" x 13"s. Following are recipes that can be prepared easily and serve many.

Creamed Potatoes

12 large potatoes, shredded or 24 oz. frozen shredded hash browns
2 cans cream of chicken soup
2 cups sour cream
1 cup grated cheddar cheese
1/2 cup chopped onions
2 cups crushed corn flakes
2 Tablespoons melted butter

Place potatoes in large bowl. Combine soup, sour cream, cheese, and onions. Stir mixture into the potatoes and pour into 9" x 13" baking dish. Spread crushed corn flakes over top. Sprinkle melted butter over corn flakes. Bake at 350 degrees for 30-45 minutes.

Potato & Meat Hot Dish

1. Spread 18-24 oz. thawed hash browns in bottom of 9" x 13" baking dish.
2. Brown 2 pounds ground beef. Drain. Add 1 can cream of mushroom soup. Spread over potatoes.
3. Shred 8 oz. cheddar cheese over meat.
4. Sprinkle crushed corn flakes on top of cheese.
5. Pour 1/4 to 1/2 pound melted butter over flakes.
6. Bake at 350 degrees for about 1 1/2 hours.

Meat & Corn Bake

(25 people)
1. Brown 4 pounds ground beef, adding 2-3 cups chopped onions halfway through browning.

2. In large bowl, mix two 1 pound cans whole kernel corn, drained; 10 oz. cream of mushroom soup; three 10 oz. cans cream of chicken soup; 3 cups sour cream; salt and pepper to taste.
3. Divide 1 pound cooked and drained noodles (or rice), into two, 9" x 13" baking dishes. Pour half the meat mixture over each, stirring lightly.
4. Combine 3 cups soft bread crumbs and 6 tablespoons melted butter. Sprinkle over top.
5. Bake at 375 degrees for about 45 minutes to an hour.

Baked Beans
(50 people)
2 gallons pork & beans
1 40 oz. bottle catsup
3/4 cup brown sugar
1/4 cup molasses
1 medium onion (minced)
1/2 pound diced bacon
1/2 tablespoon dry mustard

Bake at 350 degrees for about 1 1/2 hours.

Bean Casserole
1 large can pork and beans
1 medium can green limas (drained)
1 medium can butter beans
1 medium can kidney beans
2 onions - chopped
1 cup brown sugar
1/2 cup vinegar
1 Teaspoon dry mustard
dash garlic salt

Mix all ingredients.
Bake at 325 degrees for 3 hours. If thicker sauce is desired take lid off the last 30-45 minutes.

Sloppy Joes
(200 people)
25-30 pounds ground beef (20-25 lbs. meat per electric roaster pan, not the 9" X 13" baking dishes.)
12 bottles chili sauce
5 large bottles catsup

Green Salad With Icing
1 small package lemon jello
1 small package lime jello
2 cups boiling water
2 cups 7-up
1 #2 (20 oz.) can crushed pineapple (reserve drained fluid)
2 large bananas, sliced into small pieces
2 cups small marshmallows
Mix and let set for several hours.

Topping:
2 Tablespoons flour
1/2 cup sugar
1 egg
1 cup pineapple juice (add water to juice drained earlier)
Cook until thick, stirring constantly. Add 2 tablespoons butter. Cool mixture. Then fold 1 cup whipped cream into cooled topping. Spread over top of jello mixture. Sprinkle with chopped nuts.

Cole Slaw
(100 people)
15 pounds shredded cabbage
4 bunches celery
1 bunch carrots
1 onion

Dressing:
1 pint heavy cream, 1 pint vinegar, 3 pints Miracle Whip or mayonnaise

Potato Salad
(300 people)
50 pounds potatoes
5 dozen hard cooked and sliced eggs
1 gallon dressing
... and anything else you want in it. Olives, onions, pickles, or celery.

Cherry Cake
1. Butter 9" x 13" glass baking dish.
2. Pour two cans pie cherry filling into baking dish.
3. Empty entire box of prepared dry white, yellow, or chocolate cake
   mix over the top of cherries.
4. Pour 3/4 to 1 cup melted butter over cake mix
5. Sprinkle with nuts.
6. Bake at 350 degrees for 35-40 minutes.

Tammy's Cheesecake
Graham cracker crust:
Crush 2 packages graham crackers with rolling pin. Blend in 4
Tablespoons melted butter. Spread in bottom of 9" x 13" baking dish

Filling: Blend 2-8 oz. packages softened cream cheese with 1 cup
powered sugar. Fold in 4 cups whipped cream (2 cups unwhipped
cream). Pour onto graham cracker crust.

Topping: Spread 2 cans pie filling - either cherry or blueberry.

County Fair

County Fairs are the vacation destination of choice for rural folks, especially if they have 4-H age children or grandchildren, but also for adults who wish to enter their own projects in the open competitions.

County Fairs provide arenas for horseback riders, cattle exhibitors, demolition derby car drivers, vegetable and grain growers, politicians, and parades. Where else can ranch families spend so much quality time together? Where else can families test this spirit of togetherness?

One year, our family graduated from driving the two hour round trip to the fair grounds once a day, to parking the pickup camper for three days at the fair grounds. This meant first hauling Darryl and Todd's calves and their mothers (they were still nursing), to the fair grounds and then returning to the ranch to load the pickup camper.

While Marc finished up irrigating, the boys and I drove the cattle to the fairgrounds. Darryl and Todd tied their calves into the 4-H barn and I unhooked the gooseneck trailer, with the two bawling mother cows inside it. We drove back home to find Marc actually standing by the camper ready to load it onto the pickup.

"Hurry up, we have to enter the 4-H stuff by five o'clock."

"Okay. Okay." Marc said. "I'll take a quick shower."

Like a fire brigade, Darryl, Todd and I grabbed the piles and piles of clothes, sleeping bags, food, extra jackets, photography posters, almost ripe string beans and beets laid artistically on paper plates covered with plastic wrap, beaded bracelets, wood clocks and bowls made in shop class, and carried all of it to the camper. This vast array included Todd's prized insect collection, which he slid carefully onto the floor of the camper.

That summer, every time I had opened the freezer, I'd see another bug, flash frozen for Todd's collection. Shiny beetles of every description. Many species of flies. And the unusual, hard to find insects, like the Mormon cricket. All summer Todd, and the rest of us, were on insect alert.

We sat in the pickup waiting for Marc. He ran from the house and leaped into the back of the camper to stow his western hat. We heard an awful noise—breaking glass. The boys and I jumped out of the pickup and ran, screaming and yelling, to the camper door.

Todd stared at his precious glass-littered box of broken insects, tears streaming down his cheeks. Marc looked mortified at what he'd done. Darryl paced outside the camper and I stood bewildered, sure that our vacation and our happy togetherness was totally ruined. But time was running out. I knew we'd never make the five o'clock deadline if we stood around much longer.

I barked out orders. Darryl, fetch the Elmer's glue from underneath the kitchen counter. Todd, start picking out the glass. Marc, you drive. We'll ride in the back and try to build Rome in a day.

Once all the glass had been removed, we selected body parts that could be repaired. Todd glued the broken back of the Walking Stick together along with two of his legs, then glued the eyed head of the Click Beetle back to its winged body. We sorted other legs and heads and tried to attach them to the correct bodies. Darryl retrieved a dead fly on the window ledge to replace the mangled one. An hour later, when Marc pulled up in front of the 4-H exhibition building, we had a reasonably presentable collection.

Polly, the volunteer coordinator, greeted the boys as they lugged their projects to the table for entry tags. "Todd, what a nice group of insects you have there. But you know you're supposed to have a glass cover?"

"Yes, ma'am, I know."

The minute the exhibition door was unlocked the next

morning, Todd ran to inspect the judge's decision. The purple ribbon and comments from the judge complimenting Todd on the number of hard to find specimens in his insect collection brought smiles and much harmony back to our enclave.

Now, I thought, if we can survive the afternoon of livestock judging without further incidents, our family will truly be at peace once more. We might even vacation again next summer at the County Fair, but if Todd is still collecting insects, we'll store them up high someplace, not on the floor of the camper!

Corral Language

Cursing and cussing

Over the years as a rancher's wife, I've learned that cursing is a more serious form of cussing. I've learned how to cuss the weather when it was too hot, too cold or too windy. I've learned how to effectively cuss bankers, taxes, some unlikable people and numerous ornery beasts.

Curse words, however, are those strongest expletives used when under the most dire stress. Such as when I'm chasing our bull away from an angry neighbor's bull who broke through the fence just as I was leaving for a doctor's appointment. Curse. Curse.

Louder and louder I yell, hoping my voice will convince the marauding bull to retreat to his herd. Ding, dang it! The angry tone helps keep my spirits up as I pray my stamina outlasts this renegade. Or, maybe another person will hear my calls of distress.

Finally, reinforcements show up just as I have maneuvered the unwelcome animal back through the broken section of barbed wire fence. And our bull, exhausted and thirsty, now wanders off to the creek for a drink of water.

Animals do behave in unexpected ways. For example, the four of us once chased the cow herd out of the swampy river bottom, around the irrigated hay meadow and along the roadway leading to the corrals. We had herded them within yards of the twelve-foot wide dirt bridge that spanned the main irrigation ditch. This was just fifty feet or so from the open gate that led into the corral. But there Mr. Herd Bull stood, in the middle of the bridge, bellowing to his girls, throwing his head into the air, warning them to turn back.

Now, believe me, this unhappy predicament causes even the most modest and sedate person to let loose with a string of corral language. Ranchers develop a vocabulary of words known for their ability to intimidate. For one thing, to let that cussed bull know who's boss. So, wielding a large tree limb, I advanced forward, stepping between the pawing bull and the confused cows and let him have it right across the nose.

Satisfied that he had valiantly exhibited his leadership, the 2,500 pound bull calmly sauntered into the corral. Not certain if my corral language or the timber landing on his nose had convinced him, I jogged behind him, shouting all the way, until he was well inside the corral.

The rush of adrenalin filled me with power. I turned and ran back across the bridge, as Marc and the boys on horses moved the herd forward once again. When I reached my position on the west flank, I saw Mr. Cocky Herd Bull galloping out of the open gate, just as two more cows had crossed the bridge. Curse. It's not a matter of choice. The words escape, a valve letting off the steam of frustration.

The two cows retreated into the milling herd at the insistence of their leader. Now, pandemonium broke out everywhere.

Marc, quarter turning his horse back and forth trying to quell the pending breach, hollered, "Rachel, get that damn bull the hell out of the way."

"Shut the hell up. I did get him into the corral. Shit! Why didn't you yell when you saw his sorry ass running out of the corral?"

"Todd, run up there and help your mother. Lock the damn bull into the damn upper pen."

"I told you, Dad," yelled Todd. "This would never work! I said we ought to lock the bull up in the first place!."

"Watch your left, Darryl. She's getting ready to make a break. Hurry up! Don't you have the damn bull locked up yet?"

"You wanna trade places?" I lashed out at Marc and struck

the bull on the rump with the stick.

"Well, shit. There they go. Streaming along the irrigation ditch. You hold the rest, Darryl. My horse is faster."

"You son of a guns," I heard Marc say. "Go on. Move your sorry hides back over the bridge."

With the bull out of the way, the cows turned around and hustled into the corral.

Loud cursing also is used when a ten minute hail storm wipes out a year's alfalfa hay crop, two days before swathing. Or when your best cow calves a "mortgage payer" bull calf just before bedtime and when you check first thing in the morning and the calf is dead. There is no obvious reason for its dying.

Cussing, on the other hand, involves more common usage. Everyday words for life's smaller annoyances and perturbances. Words that you may not use in polite company but words that indicate you're not pleased. Like, "Shoot, I left the parts list on the kitchen counter. Shucks! What was I supposed to pick up in Henley?"

Or, "Doggone it, or dadblasted, or shuckydarn, or fiddlesticks, or crimeinentlies, or for pities sake, or tarnation, I'm late already. I didn't need a flat tire!"

Cursing and cussing, while perhaps not admirable skills, do serve a purpose. Ranchers tend not to grow old harboring deep-seated anger and resentments.

Oh, shoot, where did I put the bloomin' fencing pliers I was using to repair the daggone gate?

D

Dude

O h ,   b o y ,   c a n   I ?

Many dudes, young and old, visited our ranch, excited at the prospects of exchanging hectic city life for a few bucolic days in the country. Marc and I were happy to comply with their desire to take part in the daily ranch activities.

"Sure, we'd love to help tag the calves." Eagerness is written all over their smiling faces. But later—"Ooh, they smell. Yuck."

"I am leaning against him as hard as I can, Rachel, but this calf's pretty strong. Shoot. Why can't I use corral language? You do. The damn calf just stepped on my foot. It hurts. What other job can I do? I'm thirsty. When do we get to ride the horses? How many more calves are there? Are we ever going to be done? How come you didn't tag these when they were born?"

"Ouch, the stupid calf just kicked me. Ugh, his hoof had manure on it. I'm going to the house to change clothes."

"What are those stacks of boxes for in the field over there? There's bugs flying all around them. Yikes, a bee just stung me! Put mud on it from the creek? Won't I get infected from the dirty mud?"

"What's for lunch? I'm starving. We should have brought snacks. And water. How much more work do we have to do before we can go to the lake?"

After a morning of cattle duding, we offered farmer dudes a chance to realize their fondest dreams.

"Irrigating? What's that? Sure, I wanna help. Please."

"I am trying. The water won't come out of the tube. My hand's not big enough. Are you sure this is how to start a syphon? It's not working. I did not lift the tube too high. I am doing it in one smooth motion. My shoes are soaked. What kind of mud is this? It's sticking to my sneakers. The water's freezing. Can you get frostbite in the summer?

"Alright. I got one going. Look at it. Wow, this is neat. Okay, next. Wait, the water's not going down the row. What do you mean, 'dig a ditch?' Oh, that's easy. Hand me the shovel. My shovel's bouncing. Is there concrete mixed with the soil? Is it lunch time, yet?"

"Walk all the way to the end of the corn row? That must be a mile. You do this every day? Irrigating, I mean. Twice a day! Why didn't you buy a ranch where it rains? Oh, yeah, I'm having a lot of fun. When can we ride the three-wheeler?"

"Oh, goody, we get to help bring in hay."

"I have to sit in the tractor with you? Can't I drive it?

It doesn't look that hard. I can drive Mom and Dad's automatic. Five gears? No way. What's over/under mean?"

"Why are you dropping me off here? Turn the bales over? That seems awfully stupid. They can't be that wet on the bottom. Make sure all the strings are on the side, yeah, right. Rattlesnakes? There are rattlesnakes in this field? And you want me to turn ALL these bales over? Can't rattlesnakes kill a person? Especially a small person? Mom will be really upset if a rattlesnake kills me.

"Two hours, huh. You'll pick me up in two hours. Where are you going? Mowing hay. Oh, that's a cinch. Kids always get the hard jobs. Can we go fishing in the river this afternoon?"

"Something's biting me. A fly. I never heard of a fly that bites. Look, it's swelling up like a bee sting. Where's that can of spray stuff you told me to use? Do deer flies live by the river? I don't think I want to fish."

"Hey, Mom and Dad, Rachel says she'll take us to the lake after we help her in the garden. Did you know potatoes grow underneath the ground? You're doing housework? Dishes and vacuuming? Oh, ick. I'd much rather be outside."

"Isn't there some kind of poison you can spray to kill these potato beetles? Squish them with my bare hand. Unh-uh. Okay, I can flick them into this coffee can. There must be hundreds of millions of them."

"Can I trade with Rebecca now? I'd rather pull weeds. You sure have a lot of string beans. I hate string beans. Look at this. Is this a weed? It has greenish-red leaves. Beets? They grow underground, too? I wish Mom and Dad had a garden. All we have are flowers. Tons of them. They're no fun."

"This weed's easy to pull. Ouch. It stung me. Does everything in South Dakota sting? Here's a big one. Grab it near the root. Man, look at all those sand burrs. Do weeds grow better than vegetables? Is it okay to pull up a carrot and eat it? This is way funner than cleaning a dumb old house. You have to be tough to garden. Can we barbecue hamburgers at the lake? You, know, have a picnic!"

A high percentage of dudes asked about hunting. We explained that there are laws governing seasons of the year when it is permissible to hunt deer and antelope.

"But, aren't they eating your hay and grass and drinking from the river running through your property?"

"That's true," Marc replies, "but the guys working for the Game, Fish and Parks Department have to have something to do during off seasons, so they hunt illegal hunters. Tell you what though, there is one species which may be hunted 365 days a year."

"So, does that mean you'll take us hunting?"

"If you're sure you're up to it. Even though there's no limit on the number you can kill, these animals are very elusive. Jack-a-lopes are experts at camouflage. They can be hiding three yards from you and you'll never know it. Every once in awhile, though, you can catch sight of the tips of their horns. Do you still want to go on a hunt?"

"Easy. I can see the eyes of mean dogs three blocks away. I'll find one."

"Remember, even if you're lucky enough to spot one, you have to run mighty fast to catch up to them. They can out-hop a rabbit."

We returned home after two hours searching for jack-a-lopes. We saw nary a horn tip nor a hop. But we did see blooming yuccas, paint brush, and an excited seven-year-old hunter, bored with jack-a-lopes, who found a one inch Fairburn agate. Undaunted, one dedicated dude asks Marc about the animal that he heard you had to hunt with a flashlight.

"Snipes?"

"Yeah, that sounds right."

Marc thought every kid, city or country, had been on snipe hunts, but he was happy to oblige the eager youngsters.

"Tonight's a good night to hunt snipe," he told them. "There's a full moon. We might hear them howl. Rachel, do we have any snipe catching bags left?"

F

4-H Pledge

A new meaning

I pledge my heart to greater loyalty, my head to clearer thinking, my hands to larger service and my health to better living for my club, my community, my country and my world.

We signed Darryl up with the Ranching Rangers before he was officially old enough to join. He showed his first calf when he was barely tall enough to see over her back, much less control this feisty seven month old heifer.

As the years passed, Darryl and Todd loyally attended monthly meetings, prepared presentations, held offices, mowed grass in the cemetery, picked up trash in our town, and took part in County and State Fairs. All these activities gave new meaning to the 4-H pledge.

Heart to greater loyalty. This was a promise to stick by son Darryl as he practiced his "How to give a shot" demonstration, no matter how many potatoes he bruised with stabs from the hypodermic needle.

I remained loyal to son Todd, too, when he insisted that I buy five boxes of Rice Krispies and five bags of marshmallows so he could practice his demonstration on "How to make Rice Krispie treats."

When our sons decided to take part in a range management project, Marc and I even encouraged them. Little did I realize that I had just pledged my hand to the larger service of driving a hundred miles around the county to look for unique hard-to-find grasses.

And Marc pledged his hands to larger service and his head to clearer thinking when he patiently urged the livestock judging teams to clearly think about the animal. "Use your head," I often heard him say. "As you give your reasons for placing the class, clearly demonstrate that you know which animal is which and why you placed one animal over another."

My neighbor Tammy and I pledged our heart and our health to better living after we returned from our first tour of duty as chaperones for the county livestock judging team that had earned a trip to the South Dakota state fair. Clearly, I was not using my head when I agreed to take this little jaunt halfway across the state with a car full of noisy teenagers.

The first year we slept in the 4-H dorms, complete with cold water showers and kids who only required three hours of sleep. The price was right, though, so we endured. Barely. I don't think our little band of 4-Hers had ever been out of the county.

When the next fair season rolled around, Tammy and I apparently had not learned the lesson of pledging our heads to clearer thinking, as we once again agreed to chaperone the judging team. Weeks prior to leaving, however, I made arrangements for Tammy and I to stay with a pleasant older woman who rented bed space to fairgoers. We worried less about the rambunctious teens, and the team scored the highest ever in the competition.

When our children were no longer in 4-H and we watched new parents at the County Fair, we finally understood that our lives were healthier and our living better because we had been a part of the 4-H pledge.

G

Gooseneck

You can do it!

Thinking about how I learned to drive the pickup with the gooseneck trailer, I realize it was definitely a cumulative experience.

Over a fifteen-year period, I had practiced and gained a measure of proficiency in mirror checking, deer spotting, Smokey stalking, sign searching, map reading, coffee pouring, and speed nagging. I also qualified as a dog and children chaser, tire kicker and livestock looker.

And I served as a directional guide for my husband. My expertise with hand signals made him look downright clever when he backed directly under the neck of the trailer. But where was the guide during my first backing attempt? Thinking back, maybe practice backing was easier done alone. I didn't have to put up with the loud commands and laughter from those whose skills were superior.

I struggled fifteen minutes backing too far to the right, too far to the left, and then backing under, but off by an inch. Finally, I came so close—and not being a perfectionist, I slammed the ball into the slot. So, the trailer moved a little. The clamps still circled the ball.

I graduated from hooking up the trailer to actually driving the whole rig, on a trip home from a National Western Stock Show in Denver. Marc promised we would stop along the way when he was too tired to drive.

Chugging along I-25 North, past Cheyenne, Wyoming and then 85 North through Torrington, Marc continued behind the wheel while I talked and talked. I was putting myself to sleep.

"Rachel, you're nodding off again." Marc reached over and tapped my arm. "Wake up."

"Sorry, dear." I slapped my face a couple of times. "What shall we talk about?"

"Anything. I've never known you to be at a loss for words."

Three and a half hours passed with Marc driving and me talking when suddenly Marc's deep voice broke into my droning. "Rachel, do you think you can drive for awhile? The center line is moving and your talking is putting me to sleep."

I glared at him. "You actually want me to drive this thing?"

"It's easy," Marc said, as he slowed and pulled over to the side of the highway. "You aim the pickup straight down the highway and the gooseneck will follow behind." He shoved the gearshift into park and got out.

Well, why argue, I thought. I got out and walked twice around the rig, kicking tires as I went. Surely the twelve degree night air would open my eyes. I settled into the driver's seat.

"Remember. Aim straight. When you get tired, let me know. I just need twenty minutes and I'll be ready to take over."

My long and lanky husband slouched against the passenger door, using his coat as a pillow, and then cussing my short legs when I jerked the seat forward.

I paid no attention to him. I looked behind for oncoming lights. There were none. Good. I pulled onto the pavement.

"Step on the gas!" Marc suddenly yelled. "You're coming to the long hill into Edgemont."

"What hill? I don't see a hill."

"Trust me. Get the rpms up or you'll never make it to the top."

"Nag, nag, nag," I whispered as I applied more pressure to the gas pedal. Before I arrived at the top of the hill, the man was snoring.

Driving, I found, wasn't nearly as boring as being the passenger. I liked sitting behind the wheel. And the gooseneck was indeed following in behind the pickup. I smiled.

Having talked almost non-stop for hours, my mind was a void. I turned the radio on. I moved the dial back and forth for five minutes. Nothing but static. Not even Chicago or Tulsa, Oklahoma. I glanced at Marc and wondered if he had slept long enough to wake up and talk to me, but his snores discouraged me from asking.

I bit my lip. I rolled down the window for a breath of that-wake-me-up-night-air, then quickly closed it when I saw Marc scrunching into a tighter fetal position. I realigned my aching rear end to one cheek and then to the other. I drove with one hand. I drove with two hands.

Forty-five minutes passed. Marc looked so peaceful. I began experiencing heavy-eye-lid-syndrome. I drifted a bit too far to the left of center. Adrenalin surged through my body, forcing my heart to echo in my ears. I whipped back onto my side of the highway. Peering into the rear view mirror, I was pleased to see that the gooseneck stayed with me. Marc's head bounced from the back of the seat, but he didn't waken. I breathed more slowly and the heart echoes quit.

I pondered Marc's profound words of wisdom, ones I so often heard: Hit the cat! Hit the deer! Don't swerve. You'll end up in the ditch. Rachel, half our family is in this vehicle. Pull off the road if you're tired.

I eased up on the gas and geared down, which immediately brought my sleeping hubby to attention.

"W-W-What's the matter? Are you okay? Why are you slowing down?"

"I'm too tired to continue driving." I slowed to the shoulder of the road.

"Give me a minute. Guess I fell asleep. You did great, hon, I knew you could handle it."

Marc got out and walked around the gooseneck, checking the cattle on his way to the driver's door. I slid over to his warm spot, arranged my down vest behind my head and promptly fell asleep.

... and what about the backing up lessons?

I was initiated into backing the pickup and gooseneck the following January at the National Western Stock Show. Ready to head home to South Dakota, the cattle and tack were loaded and Marc drove the rig to the front of the loading dock where he parked.

"If someone wants you to move, just back the rig up and you'll be out of their way."

"But Marc...," I gulped, but I was too late. He was already on his way to the check-out office. I prayed no one would need our outfit moved. Five minutes went by. I looked anxiously for him to appear in the alley next to the office, but all I saw was the sign over the loading dock: ABSOLUTELY NO PARKING IN FRONT OF THE LOADING DOCK.

When I noticed a burly cowboy hiking straight toward our pickup, I wanted to drop to the floor, out of sight. Perhaps I could use witty conversation to stall the inevitable order, I thought to myself as I sat very still and looked out the windshield.

The cowboy leaned his long muscular body into the open window. "Say, lady, how about moving your trailer?" He wasn't smiling.

I frowned. "My husband will be here any second." I glanced down the alley. No husband.

"Can't you read the sign ma'am?" He placed his large hand on his hip.

"My husband is just checking out." I ignored the cowboy's question.

The burley cowboy looked perturbed. And big. "Oh yeah," I mumbled. "Okay, I'll back out of your way."

I slid slowly across to the driver's side. I turned the key in the ignition. The cowboy marched back to his tractor trailer and climbed inside.

I told myself I could move this huge truck and twenty-two foot stock trailer. Alright, Rachel, keep the steering wheel in place and simply reverse. I shifted. I peered down the alley again, but no Marc. I could imagine him standing in the office window watching me—and chuckling.

I stepped lightly on the gas pedal. Well, I thought it was lightly. The gooseneck took off to the left at a right angle to the pickup. I shifted into second gear and drove forward to straighten out. My heart went clunk-clunk. Now, reverse. I was gentle on the pedal and amazingly moving straight backward. My hand was steady on the wheel. So why was I suddenly jack-knifing to the right?

Okay, Rachel, let's repeat this procedure. I took a deep breath, then straightened forward, reversed backwards and jack-knifed to the left this time. I hoped the muscular cowboy could see that I was at least trying. My cheeks were turning beet red. I checked the alley again for my husband but saw instead a couple of young men standing there. Were they gawking at me?

I decided to try once more. I lined the gooseneck square to the back of the pickup. Lady Luck had to be on my side this time. I turned my head for the final reverse. Using mirrors wasn't an option.

Suddenly, I felt a hand on my shoulder. I slammed my foot on the break so hard that I could feel the cattle being thrown to the floor of the gooseneck.

"Howdy, Rachel. Having a little problem?"

"Oh, Jay, hi!" I leaped from the driver's seat. In ten seconds our young friend Jay backed the pickup and trailer to the spot I'd been trying to hit for ten minutes. I walked over and thanked him.

"Glad I could help." He sauntered off.

By the time Marc arrived, I was sitting calmly reading a book.

"I see you had to move out of that guy's way. Sorry. There was a long line at the office. Any trouble backing?"

"Nope. None at all," I lied.

Government

F a v o r i t e   t o p i c   o f   c o n v e r s a t i o n

Weather and government are two topics of conversation that spark response from even the most quiet and shy members of the ranching community.

"Why doesn't the government just get out of our business and leave us alone?" It's difficult enough to deal with adverse weather, but nothing compared to dealing with a faceless government in Washington, D.C! What do they know about our life?

Chastising the government, particularly the Federal Government is part of the culture of ranching. Why, when they slapped a beef price freeze on cattle, our market was ruined and it took four years to work our way out of that one. And then, don't forget the grain embargo on the Soviet Union. That upset the market again for years. And don't get me started on the grain Payment-In-Kind and that damn dairy sell-out or sell-down program. What were they thinking about? They certainly weren't thinking about the good ol' United States agri-industry.

We listen constantly to the glut of federal programs designed to provide jobs for the unemployed. One rancher friend said, "Let them come to my ranch. I'll be glad to pay minimum wage to anyone willing to help string barbed wire or do some clean-up work around here."

Promises. Promises. I'm suspicious of anyone offering to buy me something with another person's money. My mother-in-law says, "If the government would spend their money the way I spend mine,

I'd have no complaints." But then Mom and I didn't believe in spending on credit.

The habit of lashing out against the government becomes part of our way of life. And that's good. Whipping on the politicians saves marriages. Often I failed to understand Marc's workaholic needs, so I blamed the government.

"Why do you insist on irrigating when it's pitch dark out? You really expect supper at 11 o'clock! If the dad-blasted government would stay out of our business, you would be coming home for supper at seven like every other normal American male.

"See, if we could be left alone in a true supply and demand system our products would receive fair market value. But no, the government's always stepping in. Messing with interest rates and taxing us unfairly so that you have to work ten times harder than the city people, so we barely break even at the end of the year."

Just once I'd like to ranch without any government interference.

"But, heck, what do the government jerks know about us, anyway. Most of them are big city lawyers. They should travel to Russia and see what it's like not to have grocery stores filled and overflowing with delicious, nourishing food. And who does the government think produces all their power-packed edible proteins, anyway?"

I often blast the government for giving so much food away while we work our fingers to the bones seven days a week and no vacations. Oh, alright, I forgot about vacationing at the County Fair. Sure, how many vacations and junkets do those Washington, D.C. folks take?

"And don't get me started on taxes. Pretty soon I'll have to find a job in town to pay the taxes, and then we'll have to hire someone to do the work I do on the ranch and...oh, who cares. Stupid government! Why don't you get up earlier in the morning, Marc, so you won't have to work after dark?

There, see, I feel much better after unleashing my frustration on an impersonal government bureaucracy.

H

Husbandry

Management of domestic affairs

Taking care of the land and cattle entails thoughtful planning. So, too, does taking care of husbands. Marc's penchant for procrastination was deeply rooted within his soul. "It's part of who I am," he told me over morning coffee one day.

I never understood his need to put things off or to arrive late. I gave Marc wrist watches with alarms. I cajoled. I pleaded. I argued the rudeness of being late to which he replied, "No sense arriving before the party begins."

Meeting with the banker isn't a party, but still he rushed around like a mad man before every appointment, no matter if the meeting was at nine in the morning or three o'clock in the afternoon. There were times he failed to remember at all, though I tied a bracelet of baling twine around his wrist to jog his memory as he went about his work.

My forthrightness was met with stubborn adherence to his policy of lateness. Regardless of an event's importance, I found no convincing words to convey the meaning of 'on time.' Besides, I'm short and the view is limited from the back of churches, school gymnasiums, and town auditoriums. Eventually, however, I was forced to resort to devious means.

We were invited to the local high school play. We knew the actors and actresses. If we arrived early, I could reserve front row seats, the better for me to see and the better for Marc to hear.

That morning Marc announced he wanted to move cattle from the south pasture to the north pasture. "And while we're at it," he said, "let's move them to the corrals. There's a couple of cows I need to treat for hoof rot."

"Fine."

Couple, to Marc meant a half a dozen cows and more than likely a lump jaw or two and who knew what else. Can you help me for a couple seconds meant a couple of hours. I'll be there in a couple of minutes meant after lunch. I'll look at the broken dryer as soon as I finish a couple of jobs I'm in the middle of meant a couple of weeks.

Realizing the pasture switch, with the corral stop, would take longer than Marc figured, I executed a plan that would ensure our arrival at the school gym in plenty of time to reserve good seats. While Marc and the boys were saddling the horses, I set every clock in the house ahead, including the difficult digital clock in our bedroom. None of us wore wrist watches so I didn't need to worry about anyone checking the time while we were off working.

I filled the crock pot with beef and vegetables for our noon meal and joined my family, they on horseback and I in the pickup. The cattle walked agreeably to the corrals. No breakaways or lingering calves. We were making good time. Maybe I needn't have gone to such lengths.

Before noon—or Rachel time of 1 o'clock we sat down at the kitchen table for lunch.

"Can't be that late, can it?"

"Gosh, Marc, it did seem like things went smoothly this morning. I can't believe it's that late, either." I wandered over to the windows to close the curtains against the sun's high noon beams.

"I'm sure hungry, so maybe it just took longer than we thought."

"Yeah, that's it," I agreed.

The afternoon's work proceeded so well that we were actually back at the house by four—five Rachel time. Darryl and Todd fed the cattle in the corrals while Marc showered and shaved. He plopped onto the couch in his underwear. "I'm going to take a little snooze. Wake me in a half an hour."

I was nearly jumping for joy—we arrived right on schedule—my schedule.

"Where is everyone?" Marc asked when we walked into the empty auditorium. "Are you sure you got the time right, hon?"

"Oh, yes," I said, thankful Marc's nearsightedness prevented him from reading the clock high on the west wall. I made sure to save four front row chairs, smiling cheerfully at the regular early birds who looked totally shocked at seeing us.

"Early?" I heard him exclaim to one of the early bird's comments.

I knew I'd probably never be able to pull the clock tactic off another time—at least not any time soon.

Insects

Bite, sting, chomp and scratch

Yes, house flies, horse flies, dragon flies, flies by night and flies in the ointment, are bothersome. But on the annoyance scale, they don't come close to pesky deer flies, NSUs, gnats, red ants, chiggers, honey bees or grasshoppers.

The Deer Fly. Have you tried outrunning the deceivingly slow-moving deer fly? The female fly that lands carefully on the back of your hand, then probes her blood meal, leaving the victim with an incredibly itchy welt. Swat. Got that one. Smack. Killed her too. But there are so many.

They attack through clothing with insatiable appetites. I jump into the pickup for protection. They follow me. I step on the gas. They follow me. Or was this a new bunch? No, I'm sure it's the same group. Forty miles per hour I speed along the dirt road between pasture and hay ground. Fifty miles per hour. Six of them stay with me, hanging near the side mirror, almost in slow motion.

I bat them away. Zoom. They're back. They can't fly that fast! But here they are! I hang my arm out the window to experiment. Bingo. They land with little difficulty, immediately sensing nourishment. I roll the window tight and return to help with the irrigating down field.

I step out of the pickup and there they are, quietly absorbed in their task of surviving. I spray insect repellent on my arms and clothing. Now they hover, but keep their distance. Two deer flies zoom in close, but don't tangle with me. I make a mental note to buy a six pack of insect spray on my next trip to town.

The No See Um. NSUs or No See 'Ums, toy with my sense of reality. Noiseless specks. I sense their nearness. I feel I'm about to bump into them, yet I've never seen a live one, or a dead one, for that matter. Once in a while I observed a group, but they appeared more like a dark shadow than a physical entity with wings, heart, eyes, and mouth.

I wave my arm in front of my face. They seem to like that area of the body. Or maybe it's just that I'm aware of things when they're in front of me.

They're pesky, yet they don't drive me crazy like some other airborne insect species do. I know they aren't figments of my imagination because others have told me of their encounters with no see ums.

The Gnats. Gnats, on the other hand, are in the bothersome but not dangerous category. I see them. They do get in my face. Is body heat what they're after? My expensive perfume? My deodorant? What? Whatever attracts them to me, holds them close.

I've held my arm high and watched as they soared to the tips of my fingers, content that they had reached some sort of mountain pass or pinnacle. Then, with amazing concentration, they followed my arm as I lowered it to the side. But arms tire easily, so I tie my kerchief to the top of a long stick and point it into the air. Aha, it's not my deodorant, they swarm to the white handkerchief, billowing in the breeze.

When I wear my red baseball cap, though, they aren't the least bit interested in the button at the top of the cap, rather they tend to prefer the underside of the bill, missing often and landing in my eyes. Once I tied a long peacock tail feather to the cap. That worked until the feather swayed and fell to the side.

The arms held high has stood the test of time.

The Red Ant. The red ants living in the dry prairie lands are undoubtedly relatives of the big black ants I scorched with a magnifying glass when I was a kid in Pittsburgh. I know they exist to exact their pound of flesh in retaliation for my childhood cruelty.

Granted, they also bite Marc, our sons, neighbors and relatives, but I'm certain they go out of their way to find me. I often feel their biting pain while standing still at the edge of ant hills, during rattlesnake alerts.

I deserve to be zapped for my carelessness.

Sometimes, it was the most ordinary times they sought me out, when I was usefully engaged in weeding, checking cattle, irrigating corn rows or enjoying a sunset. Their look-outs always spotted me before I spied them.

Not even bothering to return to their hill and warn the others of the intrusion, they—and nearly always they preferred attacking me in squads—had climbed my boot, brushed by the hem of my blue jean's, onward and upward.

While bent over hoeing a patch of sand burrs—my jeans tight to my thighs—I felt the searing pain. I leapt to a standing position, calmly felt for the little ant body, grabbed it through the denim and squeezed with all my might.

Ouch, darn it! Another and another. Down came the zipper. Off with the jeans. Bright red swellings on the outside of my leg. Flick. Flick. Two down. A quick body check. Seems okay, but just in case, I do the ant dance. What did I ever do to you? I scream at them. And then I remember. I was just a kid, I yell at them.

The Chigger. Chiggers don't bother you unless you are picking plums or currents or wandering around in the brushy habitat of marshy areas. While I've suffered from chiggers burrowing into my flesh (I'm told they actually inject enzymes to dissolve skin tissue on which they feed), I've not once seen one.

Layers of tight clothing present a barrier to the chiggers who seek out their favorite warm moist spots on humans while we're invading their plumb territory. I daydream of a winter's supply of jam rather than the possibility of the worst itch imaginable caused by these mighty mites.

When my buckets are full I walk straight home, toss my clothes in the washing machine and scrub under the shower for ten minutes. Our young sons, less inclined to make a bee line to the shower after a romp in the deep bushy draws, suffered immeasurably from their lack of haste. Out comes my nail polish which they dab on each hole, thereby suffocating the little buggers.

The Honey Bee. Though small by human standards, I provide a lush target for biting and stinging insects. Even the normally peaceful honeybees seek me out. I appreciate their useful activity of pollinating the alfalfa fields. I love the honey that results from their hard labors. But I am offended that they seek out my arms, or legs, or brow.

Our bee hive colony was located within yards of the working corral. After numerous skirmishes and stinging attacks, I finally asked the bee man to kindly move the hives away from the corrals.

I pointed out Marc and Darryl and Todd to the roving bees. But they flew to the end of the chute where I was in charge of closing the head gate. I ran. They flew faster. I dodged. They zeroed in as if to say, "Only you."

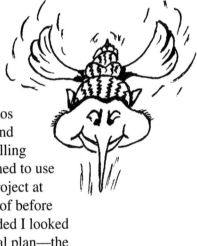

Once a bee stung me on the eyelid. I pasted baking soda to the tender area as my eye swelled shut, like a boxer who'd received a powerful right hook. Darryl took photos every day as the swelling increased, and then the days following when the swelling took twice as long to recede. He planned to use the photos for his 4-H photography project at County Fair. I nearly became a series of before and after photos. Fortunately, he decided I looked too awful and went back to his original plan—the before and after haying pictures.

The Grasshopper. The voracious appetites of grasshoppers must account for their hopping ability. I've mooshed flies, mosquitoes and bees that roamed inside the car, unable to find their way out of the open window. But grasshoppers! Open the car or pickup door, and they still won't leave. Not even my screaming when they land ka-thunk onto my arm frightens them out of the vehicle.

They crow hop, hippity hop, leap hop, fly hop, hop hop as I try to swish them out with a newspaper or magazine. Squishing small bugs is nothing to the loud crunch of a boot snuffing out a hopper. I refuse to mash a juicy grasshopper with a paper weapon. It's just too disgusting.

So, after long, freezing winters, ranchers eagerly await the warming sunshine of summer, fully aware that the warmth will awaken the insect kingdom once again.

Jerry-rig

Where there's a will there's a way

In general, jerry-rigging means using a tool to perform a task other than what the tool was designed for. Often, jerry-rigging involves baling twine or wire.

I had grained the animals, but when I dug into my jeans pocket for my jack knife to cut the twine on the hay bales, my hand came up empty.

First, I tried slipping the taut twine around the corner of the bale. No luck. After five more minutes of tugging and pulling unsuccessfully, I opted for jerry-rigging. After all, resourcefulness is admired in the ranching profession. And besides, I'm stubborn.

I grabbed the shovel—the only tool around other than a big screw driver that lay on top of the molasses bucket. But the shovel either bounced from the twine at each stroke or sunk deep into the tightly packed hay. I decided I needed more leverage, so I stood on top of an adjoining bale. Raising the shovel on high, I clenched my teeth and lowered it full steam ahead. Whack. Whack! Not one hair of the twine broke. I should have given up right then, but the art of jerry-rigging held me to the job.

I spat out a cuss word, jumped down from the hay bale, and

tried holding the twine in one hand while pummeling the string with the shovel in the other hand. Fiddlesticks, I couldn't hit the same spot twice. But jerry-riggers never give up. They make the unworkable, work. It's a matter of pride.

The bulls had finished eating their grain and were staring at me, expectantly. "Take it easy," I yelled, "I'm getting it!" I laid the shovel down and sat on the bale of hay to ponder the situation, all the while searching for a better jerry-rigging sharp edge.

I was about to give in and head back to the house to look for my jack knife, when the solution came to me. Aha—gripping the cold metal of the shovel, I sawed back and forth on the twine. Within a few seconds, I heard a pop and the hay burst apart. I smiled. I laughed out loud. I sang joyous melodies while spreading out slabs of green, sweet smelling alfalfa to the waiting cattle. I knew my place in the jerry-rigging hall of fame was assured.

Loans

Levels of commitment

Lend me your ear involves commitment, same as lend me your money. It's the payback that's different. Borrowing money from a bank requires that you already have money in the bank equalling the amount you wish to borrow. Or that you have collateral (sheep, hogs, cattle, machinery, paid up deed to your ranch, a trained cow dog, a winning race horse, a spouse working in town for a generous employer, or wealthy parents who named you in their will), that exceeds the amount for which you've applied.

Loaning a piece of equipment requires that you barter your labor or part of the crop in trade. This is an even-up loan. Ranchers also place their loans of equipment and labor in escrow accounts.

For instance, when Dillon's burst appendix required emergency surgery and recuperation time, neighbors lent their equipment and labor to finish bringing in his first cutting of alfalfa hay. This is an open-ended loan, whereby the rancher lays away his efforts in escrow, so to speak, to be drawn out on a day down the road when he is laid up from back surgery or recuperating from a nasty spill off a horse.

Then there's loaning your support to an organization, which usually is not a matter of merely writing a check. Living in an area where cattle outnumber people, it's bodies that most organizations need. Folks to sell raffle tickets. To fry hamburgers. To assist 4-H-ers with projects and to attend educational meetings on predator control, the proposed tax bill or the beef check-off.

The word loan suggests that the something borrowed will be returned. In the case of bank loans, it's an eye for an eye, cash for cash. Clearly no room for creativity here. And yet, to be certain of no misunderstanding, bankers create a plethora of paperwork—forms listing and detailing and itemizing one's assets and liabilities, with plenty of room for numerous signatures declaring the legalities of the transaction.

In day-to-day ranching, however, folks verbally agree to loan feed until the next load of oats comes into the feed store. Or loan vehicles—four-wheel drive pickup owners are often appreciated by two-wheel drive pickup owners, or work loans—I'll preg check your cow if you'll help me vaccinate mine.

Loaning an ear, like listening, sympathizing, and now and then offering a solution, is a prime rate bargain. A shoulder to cry on or a person to laugh with are loans reciprocated many times over. Loans that money can't buy.

Ranchers are committed to each other just as strongly as they are committed to their job of raising cattle.

M

Mechanical Malfunctions

And other moving violations

The baler broke down one time after only two rounds of the field and rain was forecast for late afternoon. The heater in the pickup once decided to spew cold air in mid-January as the temperature dropped to zero degrees. And our unfaithful VW bug malfunctioned so often that Marc welded a tow bar permanently to the front end of the vehicle. My mother-in-law and I carried drinking water during the summer months, and extra gloves, caps and coats during the winter months, for the inevitable hike down a neighboring rancher's lane in search of a telephone.

Exasperating as those malfunctions were, though, nothing compared to the malfunction that occurred on one of my husband's livestock hauling trips.

Marc agreed to haul his brother's cow to the vet's for a pregnancy check. Not wanting to break his record of never missing a noon meal, Marc first loaded the cow and then stopped by the house to eat dinner before continuing on into town.

Peacefully snoozing after lunch, we were jolted awake by the loudest rumbling and thundering noise we had ever heard. We peered out the living room window. We didn't see any disturbance. Not even a sign of a sudden wind storm. Next, we ran to the kitchen.

Yikes! The pickup and the gooseneck trailer had crashed through the kitchen door, splintering the wood door jam and knocking huge chunks of plaster from the wall. We ran out the side door and around the house to check the damage. The cow was fine. The pickup was not. Nor was the house.

Marc pried wood from the front bumper while I hunted down a pole to jerry-rig what was left of the upper door jam to keep it from totally collapsing as he backed the pickup out of the doorway.

"Way to go," I muttered. I stared at the wreckage, thankful

the cow was okay and that the damage to the pickup didn't look too severe after all.

"Oh, be quiet," Marc growled as he stared at the wreckage. "How on earth did this happen?"

"Well, my dear husband," I began, "Let's see ... wasn't it you who cautioned us, NEVER EVER park a loaded gooseneck on a slope? Yes, I do believe it was you."

"I always knew my need for food would get me into trouble one day."

"Food, umm. Methinks more likely you forgot to set the hand brake. You know how easily that pickup slips out of park."

"Oh, you're really loving this, aren't you?"

"Yep!" I couldn't help it. I broke out laughing.

The bumper had absorbed most of the shock, so the pickup survived the impact without too much structural damage. But the house—wow! It was a mess. This was no laughing matter.

Three weeks passed with no attempt by my dearly beloved to clear the doorway wreckage. We entered and exited the house through the less convenient side door. Bugs and breezes came in through the kitchen door, despite Marc's effort to close the hole with a flimsy plastic tarp. My complaints about the path of dirty boots across the living room rug created no sense of urgency to repair the damaged doorway.

Marc's brother, a superior jerry-rigger, brought his crow bar and come-a-long over one afternoon and uncrinked the frame, enough so the door would close. Never mind the gaps where the air and bugs still crept through. Marc wasn't bothered by the mess. He didn't seem to mind walking around to the side door. More weeks passed, turning into months.

Neighbors sharing a meal with us, chided Marc about not fixing the house. I threatened him with the 'expensive repair man' ploy. I had to back down, though, because I knew we didn't have the extra money for house repairs.

Looking at the wire mesh, bare of plaster or wall board, stirred my resentment. "You got the pickup repaired immediately!" I thundered. "Why not the house? You love the darn cows more than me." It had been months since I'd tried that refrain.

This brought a response, but unfortunately, one that I had heard too often. "Yeah, yeah, okay. I'll take a look at it." Within weeks, I knew winter would be upon us.

I designed a banner to hang over the ugly wire. On it I pinned HAPPY THANKSGIVING, then MERRY CHRISTMAS and HAPPY EASTER, and later HAPPY SUMMER, and still later, HAPPY BIRTHDAY, RACHEL.

"Oh, quit nagging," moaned my husband. "You know we're in the middle of haying season. Anyway, you should appreciate the breeze on these hot days."

On the first anniversary of the pickup/door collision, I created a collage of ribbons and paper flowers, poking them into the mesh wire. We toasted the event and sang songs.

I think Marc was at last nudged into action when he saw the HAPPY THANKSGIVING banner go up for the second time. Or, maybe it was the snow piling up on the kitchen floor that convinced him the time had come to repair the doorway and wall. Two afternoons of sawing and nailing, and the job was done.

"Well, I sure thought it would be a bigger job than that," Marc said. "Here, Rachel, I bought you a little something while I was in town getting the supplies." From behind his back he brought out a gorgeous bouquet of flowers and thrust them into my arms.

O
Office

In the main ranch office where the wood stove resided, as well as the washing machine and dryer, stood a big green metal desk we had retrieved from the dump. Also, a three-drawer steel file cabinet and one cardboard file box. A rickety wooden chair that once lived out in the barn, served the desk area and the ancient electric typewriter on its stand next to the desk.

The secondary office was sandwiched into a 2' X 2' wall space that held both the wall telephone and a large Do It All Insurance calendar. Notes, messages, telephone numbers, names and addresses—scribbled on bits of paper or on the calendar—were always tucked behind the phone, on the widow sill, or jumbled on the small counter, all within reach of the telephone.

This sanctuary was primarily Marc's office and wasn't to be disturbed by a neat-freak wife. "Rachel," he scowled one day, "where in the heck is that piece of paper I wrote the guy's name down who needs 15 bulls?"

"I don't know. I didn't touch anything."

"Then where is it? If you lost that number, it could cost us a lot of money. I just had it right here." Marc pointed, as though his finger would make the missing scrap of paper magically appear.

I interrupted my bread kneading to lend a hand. Actually, to be perfectly honest, I did remember moving a couple of crumbled up scraps of paper. I poured Marc a fresh mug of coffee and suggested he take the load off his feet. As soon as he was out of sight, I quickly sifted through the waste basket and found a coffee stained teeny, weeny, dogeared empty matchbook that had several indistinguishable numbers written on it. "Is this it?" I asked innocently.

"Whew! Where did you find it? I looked everywhere."

"Oh, it was on the floor. You probably accidentally brushed it off in your mad searching."

So, although my husband's wall office was in a constant state of disarray, I learned to live with it. Bull sales are our livelihood. I took over eighty percent of the army-green metal desk, donating twenty percent to Marc, with the promise that I wouldn't touch his stuff.

I didn't mind the tedious bookwork. My memory wasn't as advanced as Marc's so I wrote lists and organized papers into file folders. During periods of slow cash flow, stacks of envelopes and papers arose and spread, threatening my peaceful neatness.

Even some of Marc's plan-to-look-at-when-I-have-a-free-moment magazines, newspapers, and assorted advertisements started creeping over to my side of the desk.

"That's my half of the desk." I stomped my foot. "It's time to sort and throw stuff out."

"Oh, picky, picky," Marc said. "Neatness isn't a virtue, you know."

"I can't even find the bills," I moaned.

"Nag. Nag. So buy a couple of those in/out boxes."

Our office became a war zone. I became territorial. And Marc grew impatient. Then he sold a dozen commercial bulls. The bill pile disappeared, thus inspiring Marc to read and sort, until what remained would again fit in his three stacking baskets. I breathed a sigh of relief and we called a truce. Until next time!

P

Parts/Machinery

W h a t   I   d r o v e   t o   t o w n   f o r

As an action verb, the word parts means to separate. As when a horse stumbles, and the rider parts company with his or her mount, crash landing into a patch of low-growing cactus.

Parts, as an adjective, describes a far distant place. For instance, "If I have to endure another week of twenty-five below zero weather, I'm leaving for parts unknown." Unknown because I didn't know which part of the car would break down or which part of the state I'd be in when that happened.

The noun, however, refers to items, parts whose repair or replacement is critical to a smooth running machine.

I planned a trip to the Big City, sixty miles north of our ranch, to do major food shopping at the Low Cost Bulk Grocery store. Knowing the grievous consequences of the sin of omission (driving to the Big City twice in one day), I asked Marc if he needed anything.

"Yes. Stop by the bearing place and pick up enough grease to repack the two front tractor wheels. Oh, yeah, and pick up the new bearings, too."

"How many and what size?"

"The parts guy will know. Just tell him it's for a 4020 John

Deere. And I could use a half a dozen of those long bolts. You know, the ones we use to build the wind break? They're about, let's see, 8-10 inches, with the round heads.

"Which? Eight or ten? Are these the bolts that once you pound them in, you can't pull them out. The ones with the tiny threads on the end?"

"Those are ring shank nails, my dear. Remember hammering them when we repaired the corrals? They were tough as, well, nails. I'm talking about carriage head bolts. I'm not sure how long they are. You'll have to measure one. I think there's one on the shop counter.

"Anything else?"

"Yeah. How about bringing back a handful of shear pins for a 276 New Holland square baler. And while you're there, you may as well pick up 4 more bales of twine. By the way, have you seen the vice grips? I haven't seen them since I used that one pair to hold the belt tensioning arm on the swather. They're a pretty good price out there at the surplus store."

"Where?"

"On the way to airport. I forget the road name, but you turn at the gas station corner just as you come into town, head east a few miles, and after you cross the railroad tracks, look for a big warehouse-looking building to the north of the highway. You can't miss it.

"Do you have a second? You may as well get the part I need for the stack wagon. You can get the parts at the same place as the shear pins while you're in town. Come on outside. I'll show you what I need."

So much for spending an hour or two at the newly-opened mall. Amazingly, the bearing man knew exactly what I was talking about, but he was sorry he'd sold the last of the size I needed an hour ago. "Don't worry, ma'am. Have a seat and help yourself to a cup of coffee while I make a few phone calls. I might be able to rustle you up some from John's Bearings."

I knew I should have packed a book along. I picked up a three-month old Popular Mechanics from the eclectic assortment of tattered magazines scattered on the bench next to the parts counter.

Twenty minutes passed like an hour.

I strolled up to the counter. Bob had the telephone crooked between his chin and shoulder while he leafed through a half a dozen parts books. "Yeah, I know we've got what you want. Yep, it's going to be a scorcher today..."

I coughed, trying to grab Bob's attention. "Be right with you, ma'am. Okay, here we go, George. This is it. I can give you a real good price if you buy a box. I'll set it aside. This afternoon will be fine. So long."

"Can I help you? Oh, yes, I was checking on bearings for you. Tell you what. We're really busy right now. Do you have other errands you need to run? Why don't you stop back after lunch?"

Great. That was a wasted half hour. On to the twine.

"What do you mean it comes in 9000 or 20,000 foot? My husband didn't mention any lengths. It's for a square baler."

"Do you want plastic or sisal?"

How stupid of me. I should know the answer to this one. Plastic, that's it. Plastic so the mice can't chew through the strings. You can't burn the darn stuff, unless you have a huge hot trash fire so it melts down.

"Yes, plastic. Let me see the boxes. Then I can tell which length." I wanted out of this store quick. "Give me a handful of sheer pins, too, would you?" I said casually.

"What model baler?" The parts man stared through me.

"I remenber. Wait, I wrote this down." I fumbled for my part's list. "It's a 276 New Holland."

"Oh, and I almost forgot. We need a part for the stack wagon. It's that little whidge-a-ma-hicky that goes to the pull handle." The parts man looked at me with disapproving eyes and I heard a whispered comment in the parts stacks about wives and parts.

"Well, let me get my book out. What model is it? Don't get upset. Maybe if you see the picture you'll recognize your stacker. Is it this one? How many bales does yours hold?"

"I don't know, I think there's sixty-nine bales in a stack. No, that picture doesn't look like the right one." Darn, why didn't I ask Marc for the part number he wanted replaced!

The man flipped past pages of schematics showing gear boxes and hydraulics, until he came to the page with a picture of a stack wagon. He turned the book toward me. "Does this look familiar," he asked. I heard snickering in the back.

"That looks like ours, I think." I pointed to the general area that Marc had earlier pointed out to me. "See that thing-a-ma-jig right there by the whatcha-ma-call-it? I'm sure that's the part he needs." Sweat is pouring from my underarms. I swear I'm going to buy a Polaroid camera so I can take a photo of the indescribable part. If Marc would file those books that come with the equipment, I wouldn't be standing here looking like a fool.

"Here, ma'am," he handed me the telephone, "get your husband on the phone, so we can find out what it is you're looking for."

The thought occurred to me that from now on, Marc should do the food and parts shopping and I'll sit on the tractor.

"Hi, honey. The guy says I need a model number for the stack wagon. Yes, I've seen ours, but I didn't notice the model number. Okay, got it. Yes ... yes, dear. Yes, I know you told me the number, but I forgot to write it down."

I drove away from the Big City much later than planned, swearing to save up money to buy a Polaroid camera.

"Hi honey." Marc was standing in the driveway when I pulled onto the yard.

"What?" I saw the look.

"One of the baler needles busted. I called the dealer. He'll have it setting on the counter for you."

Peacocks

The best gift ever

One year I decided that I wanted to buy Marc a memorable Christmas gift. Not another flannel shirt or brown western belt or pair of long underwear or the package of six various-sized screw drivers. I wanted to find a gift so surprising that he would still be talking about it the following Christmas.

A registered Polled Hereford heifer calf would fit his description of memorable, of course, but it wouldn't fit my pocketbook. November neared and not one memorable idea presented itself. And then I thought about how he admired Tammy and Chuck's peacocks. Yes, I would surprise my rancher husband with a pair of gorgeous birds!

I made arrangements with Tammy, and the day before Christmas, drove over to their place just before dark.

Every evening Tammy's flock of peacocks strolled into the chicken house to eat cracked corn and roost the night away on the rafters. Quietly, we sneaked into the peacock motel. I held a burlap bag open while Tammy swiftly covered an unsuspecting peacock with a fish net attached to a long pole.

One down. The rest of the birds, now alert to the menace of two humans invading their sacred space, began flying back and forth across the length of the coop or scurrying underneath the hen nesting boxes. Swoop. Tammy missed.

"Rachel, start crowding them into that corner. Go easy."

I startled one dull-colored female, and she took wing right by my head, causing me to duck and yell, "There she goes." This startled the entire group of 16 peacocks, who beat their way to the opposite end of the coop.

"Slow and steady," said Tammy. "Let's try again."

Swish. Tammy concentrated on holding the net tight to the ground as I brought the burlap sack. "In you go," she spoke soothingly to the second bird. "Are you sure Marc will be pleased about this noisy little surprise, Rachel?"

"Oh, yes! It'll knock his socks off." I laid the now quiet burlap bundles gently into the trunk of the car and closed the lid. As I swung into our driveway I saw Marc walking towards the house.

"Where've you been?" he asked.

"Tammy's. I dropped off the Christmas cookies.

"Well, I'm heading out to chore."

"Take your time."

When Marc was out of sight I carried the burlap bags out to the chicken coop and released them. I set out water and feed, praying the new surroundings wouldn't provoke the birds into the typical loud, alarming peacock cries for help.

On Christmas morning we opened our gifts before morning chores. Darryl and Todd oohed and ahhed over their new long johns, snowmobile boots, books and battery operated airplanes. Marc surprised me with a hooded pink winter jacket, one too pretty to wear for chores.

"Your gift is outside," I said excitedly.

Darryl and Todd struggled to contain their enthusiasm. "Yeah, Dad, wait until you see what Mom bought you. You're never going to believe it!"

"A four-wheeler?" Marc always thought big.

We pulled on our winter jackets for the trip outdoors. Marc played along. "What could you possibly get me that's outside? Must be something that's too big to fit inside."

"Come on, Dad," Todd called. "This way." He led us toward the chicken coop where earlier in the year I had raised a hundred Cornish Rocks, now in the freezer.

The boys slowed as they neared the coop.

"Is it hidden in there?" Marc frowned. "I sure hope not." He looked nervous. I smiled. "You better not have bought me chickens, Rachel. You know how I hate chickens. They're messy, diseased, smelly, foul birds."

"You never mind eating them."

"Nope. But, if you bought me chickens this will be the last day alive for them."

"Okay, Dad. I'll unlatch the door so you can look for your present."

"Wait...aren't the rest of you coming in? I'm not going in there alone."

"Dad," Darryl said, "no one said there's chickens in there. Come on. Take a look."

Marc held the door open a crack, just wide enough to determine that I really hadn't bought chickens. "Peacocks!" he exclaimed. "You gave me peacocks. Are they a pair?"

"Near as Tammy and I can figure. Do you like them? Are you surprised? Is this the best gift ever?"

"Yes, I can say it's definitely a present I won't forget." He swung his arm around my shoulders as we walked back to the house. "I wonder how many grasshoppers they can eat."

Pets

Inside, outside.

Marc's folks raised five kids in a series of three small houses. Maybe that's why they didn't have indoor pets. Maybe they figured the house was for people and the great outdoors was for animals. So why Marc was soft on house pets I never figured out.

Elkhounds, a dog breed suitable to living their entire lives outdoors, bounded throughout our house. The first elkhound we owned even snuck onto the couch after we turned in for the night. I discovered his secret once when pregnancy hunger woke me in the middle of the night and I came downstairs for a snack. Come morning, though, Cappy was sound asleep on the rug. Only a collection of dog hairs remained on the sofa as evidence of his sneaky behavior.

Marc and I barely tolerated Todd's cat, Explorer, in the house. We caved in only when the boys begged to let her in on nights when the temperature dropped below zero.

"That cat's not coming in when she's pregnant, though!" I said, "I don't care how cold it is outside."

Todd and Darryl knew better than to argue with me.

Yet, for some unknown reason, Marc tolerated the boys' pet rodents. Those disgusting gerbils did nothing but breed, breed, shred egg cartons, breed, chomp carrots, breed, zoom around their tunnels and breed some more.

The gerbil fixation was the fault of Darryl and Todd's cousin Trevor who asked us to babysit his two pet gerbils for a weekend. "No problem," we agreed. After all, how much looking after does a gerbil need?

We found out that weekend that all the egg carton shredding raised the possibility for escape. The first morning I padded barefoot into the kitchen to brew coffee and saw the adorable little rodent rummaging through the garbage can. "Eek!" I shrieked. I swished him into a paper bag, dumped him back into his cage and tossed in a fresh carrot.

That night, about midnight, I heard a scratch, scratch sound from under our bed. "Marc," I yelled, "there's a mouse somewhere in this room. GET HIM OUT OF HERE!"

"Oh, go to sleep. It's probably a twig scratching on the window outside."

I peered out the window. "No, can't be...there's no wind."

I climbed back into bed, putting my sneakers on the end of the bed. I wasn't taking any chances of a rodent nesting in my shoes.

"Honey, you hear that?" I elbowed Marc. He raised his head from the pillow. "I'll bet one of those dumb gerbils is loose."

Our investigation proved that both of the little devils were chewing away on the Christmas paper under the bed.

"Okay," Marc said, "Grab that empty waste basket and bring the broom so I can scooch them your way."

I grabbed the yard stick from our closet. "You hold the waste basket. I'll do the scootching."

But they were speedy. Marc leaped off the floor when one of them missed the waste basket and zoomed between his naked legs. "Time out!" I said. I giggled.

On my third try I slowly moved the yard stick parallel to the floor making sure the gerbils were between the stick and the trash basket. "Here they come," I said quietly. "Get ready. You'll have to be quick." They were within inches of waste basket. "Come on little guys. Keep moving toward the basket."

Thinking they were closer than they were, I swooped the stick behind them intending to tap their little behinds into the waiting trap. Instead, I whopped one small butt a bit too hard. He squealed, scaring his mate and Marc who jumped up and threw himself onto the bed.

A dozen tries in the next 30 minutes finally netted the gerbils. They slid easily from the slippery plastic waste basket into their aquarium tank home.

"You're real smart," I heard Marc call from the boys' bedroom. "No wonder they escaped. You let the egg carton scraps build up to the edge of the tank."

Kind cousin Trevor bequeathed two more gerbils from the next litter to our sons who spent hours watching them build their tunnels and their nests. Amazingly, the boys were able to strike a deal with the local pet shop owner, who bought all the unwanted young from the prolific pair.

When we moved from Pennsylvania to South Dakota, Marc and I convinced Todd, age 5, that the neighbors would provide a very good home for Cally, the cat. We didn't, however, locate anyone willing to take the gerbils off our hands, so they made the seventeen-hundred mile trip to South Dakota with us. Along with Cappy, the elkhound, and a white rabbit Darryl found the night before we left Pennsylvania.

Seven-year-old Darryl spotted this pitiful creature in our pasture just before bedtime. "Dad, he's so tame," Darryl said as he stroked the soft fur.

"Ick! Don't touch it!" I said. "It's probably diseased. Why else would someone turn it loose on our farm?"

"Ah, Mom, he's so cute." Darryl released the critter on the bare living room floor. But the rabbit didn't move, other than to lay his head down.

"That's it," I said. "Whoever did this, is cruel. Dumping off a sick rabbit. Darryl, look at him. He'll be dead by tomorrow. Better to put him out of his misery now."

Marc stared in disbelief. Todd put his hand out to pet the

rabbit. I grabbed his hand. "Don't touch it. I'm not kidding. Something's definitely wrong with him."

"Dad, please?" Darryl knew the real softy in our family. Macho Dad. Dad, the same man who grew up with people inside and pets outside.

Knowing he'd penetrated through Dad's outward tough-guy image, Darryl pleaded again. "Come on Dad...give it a shot or one of the pills you give the cattle. You always make them better."

I feared this was a winning argument.

"No way," I continued, "we're not taking a dumb rabbit seventeen-hundred miles across country with a dog that wants to devour both him and the stupid gerbils. No!" I sensed I was fighting a losing battle.

Darryl ignored me. "How's this for an idea? Give him a shot of penicillin, Dad. It wouldn't take much. You could use one of those tiny needles you use when a cow gets pink eye. Mom thinks he'll be dead by tomorrow, anyway, so what will one shot hurt?"

Marc glanced at me. I shot him a firm look and shook my head. "Well, I guess I could give him an eighth of a cc of penicillin. But Darryl, don't go getting attached to him. Mom's probably right. He looks sicker than 1 dose of penicillin. Kill it or cure it, the vet used to tell me."

Darryl woke me before the alarm did. "Mom! Hey Dad...guess what? The rabbit's alive! I'm going to name him Whitey. You should see him. He's hopping all over the living room floor. And he likes dog food. Thanks, Dad. See, Mom, he wasn't that sick."

"Wash your hands," was all I could think to say that was appropriate for a small child's ears.

Cappy, the Norwegian Elkhound, and Todd rode in the big truck with Marc. I shared the VW bug with Darryl, two gerbils and Whitey. Darryl plied his shy smile when he begged waitresses for carrots and lettuce. "Oh, how sweet," they would say. I held my tongue.

Our odd entourage arrived in South Dakota after an uneventful three-day trip, tired and anxious to stretch our legs, but none the worse for the wear. Marc's folks, who had moved to South

Dakota the month before, greeted us warmly and offered iced tea and sticky buns.

Cappy bounded out of the truck and ran off to sniff his way around the barn and corrals. Darryl carried Whitey to Grandmom's green lawn for a feast of fresh grass.

Leaving the rabbit happily munching, Darryl came in for a sticky bun before hurrying back to his new pet. But it was too late. The elkhound had already torn into Whitey as though the rabbit were a fearsome ground hog. Darryl ran to Grandmom's basement bedroom where he cried himself to sleep. Time, not my offer to comfort him, would ease a small boy's pain.

As heartbreaking as the Whitey incident was, Darryl fortunately had not truly attached himself to the rabbit. The next day he and Todd and Cappy hiked all over the five-hundred-acre ranch, exploring the hillsides for shell fossils and Fairburn agates.

No more pets entered our life until the following summer when Todd made friends with a butterfly. For a brief two weeks we shared our house with an inside/outside pet butterfly.

Todd spied the bright orange and black monarch flitting among the zinnias. Slowly, he slid his finger under the legs of Mr. Butterfly until he was secure. Then, talking calmly to this small, but beautiful creature, Todd walked into the house.

"Look at my pet butterfly, Mom." Mr. Butterfly walked along Todd's hands as though they were familiar territory. I stared in amazement.

Aware of Todd's rich imagination, I didn't see the point in arguing that butterflies aren't pets, especially since the monarch had just flown from Todd's hand to land on the multiflowered dining room curtain.

With the sureness of a child, Todd soaked a napkin in syrupy sugar water and wrapped it around a pencil. Standing on the dining room chair, he reached the sweet pencil up to the butterfly who immediately latched onto it and began feeding.

Mr. Butterfly spent the night in the house, flying back and forth between the flowered curtains and stopping for nips on the sugar coated napkin that Todd had propped up in a glass. The next day Todd decided to take his butterfly outside for nature's nectar.

As a disbelieving adult, I suggested that the butterfly would probably fly away. "Don't expect too much," I warned. Gently, Todd held his butterfly next to a tall orange zinnia. He watched for a while, then came inside for lunch.

"Don't you want to bring your butterfly in?" I worried over how disappointed he'd be when the butterfly flew away.

"Mom, he's my friend. He won't go anywhere."

Two hours later, Todd fetched his monarch from the flower bed. I couldn't believe my eyes—Todd walked up to Mr. Butterfly, placed his finger next to his tiny legs and the butterfly hopped aboard.

We shared the small boy's joy as he herded his winged pet in and out of the house for the next two weeks. I was surprised that Todd wasn't upset the day Mr. Butterfly flew off toward the river. "Don't worry, Mom, maybe he's leaving to find a mate."

I hugged my six-year old and said, "You're probably right."

Photography

A p i c t u r e ' s w o r t h a 1 0 0 0 w o r d s

Snapping photographs of cattle aggravates not only the animal, but the photographer and the photographer's helpers as well. At least a thousand words—most of them unkind to the animal, the photographer and the photographer's helper—are dispensed during a session of live animal photography.

Marc, so patient while training me to drive the tractor, or teaching me how to administer medication to a cow, or helping a newborn calf learn to nurse, never mastered photo-patience. He thinks that a photographer is a person who walks out into the pasture of calmly grazing animals with his handy-dandy automatic camera. Point and shoot. Presto. You've snapped a perfect photo.

"Holy cow! This is a terrible picture...did you take that one, Rachel? Look at the bull's head. Looks like its ten sizes bigger than real life. And this one...." He pointed to a photo of Miss Sunshine.

"How in tarnation can we show her perfect udder when her hind leg is in the wrong position!"

Each year we advertised in the breed publication. And each year I pushed for an early deadline for the task of setting up our ad. Both of us understood the value of a bull's photograph to promote our breeding program. We also recognized that using a poor photo was worse than no photo at all. Once, unable to capture the perfect stance of a bull by deadline date, we actually laid out an ad with just our address and telephone number.

Aware of the guaranteed stress factor, neither of us looks forward to the annual picture taking day. We easily remember last year's exchange of angry barbs, similar to the words recently exchanged as we prepared our yearly income tax figures. The perfectionist side of Marc clashes with my 'it's good enough' side.

My husband first insists on washing all traces of manure from the bull's shedding hair coat, blowing the animal dry, and then clipping hair from the belly, the head, the shoulders and anywhere else that his eye sees a need. By the time the bull is groomed, the sun is at noon position, a photographer's worst light. But the bull won't remain clean for long, and the sooner we complete this odious job, the sooner we can return to pleasant communication.

"Hold the darn bull still," I yell. First, we try halter shots, which rarely work to our satisfaction. Then finally we agree on turning the bull loose in the corral for the 'natural' pose. Of course the bull gallops towards the gate leading to his brood cows or he crosses the pen to the wood slab windbreak for a good rub. He definitely does not stand still. And he doesn't stay clean and beautiful.

"Can't you move him away from those unsightly boards? There, that's close enough. Okay, now whistle. Get him to hold his head up. Great."

"Hurry up!" Marc, the perfectionist, hisses at me. "Take it. Now. Oh, too late. He's taking a pee. Get ready. I'll move him around again."

"That's it," I yell. "Just get his back leg right." Click. Click. I fire off a couple of perfect shots and then notice that the huge cottonwood tree in the background will look like it's growing out of his back. "No good."

"Ah, come on, Rachel, look through the daggone lens, would you!"

"Listen Superman, why don't you take the pictures and I'll move the bull around!"

"At least I'd snap the picture at the right moment."

"Yeah, 'cause I'd do a better job of setting up the bull. Don't be so impatient."

"Impatient! We've been working at this stupid picture taking for twenty minutes. How much time do you need to snap one decent photo?"

"Well, don't maneuver him where the chute's in the background or where he's in front of that cottonwood tree."

"For crying out loud, Rachel, I'll worry about my job. You worry about yours."

"You spent hours washing and clipping the gosh-darned animal, but you can't spend a few minutes taking his photograph."

"I hate this part. I told you I'm lousy around photography."

"So, what am I supposed to do? Take the picture by myself? Without any help? Well...fine...leave me be, but don't complain when the print isn't exactly what you want."

And that's how it went every year. Shadows and trees in the wrong places. Weeds in the photo that looked like extra parts on the bull's underside. Tails and noses that were in the frame when I snapped the shutter but somehow disappeared from the negatives.

One warm late spring day, son Todd, also a perfectionist, joined our annual photography nightmare of near misses and more than a thousand words of corral language.

"Do you and Dad argue like this every year?"

"Yep," we both replied.

"You'll never shoot good photos. Here, give me the camera, turn the bull out to pasture where he's content, and I'll take the pictures."

And so we did. And happily, more often than not, we met the breed publication deadline with a better than average shot of Mr. Herd Bull.

Pity Party

Table for one

Guests at Pity Parties aren't welcome. They have been known to spoil the sodden atmosphere with their laughter, or worse, with their reasoned logic. Though I've attended indoor Pity Parties, they aren't nearly as satisfying, due to the risk of nosey intruders. Therefore I recommend this function take place out-of-doors, in the wide open space of pastures, preferably during warm weather.

Sub-zero freezing temperatures tend to shorten the sessions, freezing both tears and nose dripping which ruins the drama of the totally self-indulgent nature of the Pity Party. Since the occasion generally lasts for hours, holding it on a warm summer's day is more sensible.

I'm sure there are those who prepare for their unique Pity

Party for days, but I prefer spontaneity. The right moment strikes and off I go with a thermos of coffee and a box of tissues or a roll of toilet paper.

I don't have a favorite destination, so each long walk covers different territory. For instance, I've sat by the dugout under the shade of Russian Olive trees, contending with flies and mosquitoes. I've meandered through the cow herd to plunk myself down on the river bank where pet cows interrupt my stream of consciousness. There is no wrong setting, provided it is out of ear shot of other human beings who might threaten the success of such an important feeling-sorry-for-myself endeavor.

There isn't one specific trigger that sets me off on my annual journey. Rather, I believe the cause tends to be cumulative. Physical exhaustion often leads to emotional exhaustion. Unbidden, tears well up, as though they've been filling the lake behind a dam and now simply must spill to prevent further erosion of one's self-esteem.

Crying is definitely therapeutic. Not only the stream of tears draining from eyes straining little from the effort, but also tears accompanied by great expressive sobbing. A heaving from the soul. Choking that creates shortness of breath. And a steady dripping from the nose.

At the same time I attain my peak crying mode, I've also sunk to my lowest, most depressed level. Therein lies the secret for success. The staccato choking subsides. The tears turn to sniffles. And from my mouth pour words shouted at decibels high enough to silence bird songs and send frightened calves to hide by their mothers' sides.

My torrent of pitiful words are aimed at Marc, of course, the perceived bad guy.

You knew how excited I was that my brother was coming for a visit. And how I'd planned the picnic by the lake. But did you care? No. You had important things to take care of. Like haying. I swear it wouldn't matter when I planned something, you'd find a way to sabotage it.

Remember when I bought tickets for the playhouse? I reminded you weeks in advance. And that night, what happened? A stupid heifer decides to calve. Could we figure she'd have it on her own. Oh, heck no. We did that once. We left a heifer that you didn't think was that close and she calved and the calf was dead when we checked her after the movie, so naturally we'll never leave a heifer alone again.

The gods conspire against me. I'm not blaming you entirely...well, actually I do blame you. But I want to understand. To feel worthwhile. What about when you are late? Oh, shoot, that's all the time. Boy, do you know how to annoy me.

And how is it that the cattle always have their needs fulfilled? When I'm reincarnated I'm returning as one of your cows. Then, I know I'll get the attention I deserve. I mean, come on, Marc, what did I ever do to become so unimportant. You love the cows more than you love me. You must. You sure as heck spend more time with them. You don't love me!

When I holler those words out loud, alone with the cows in the far pasture, they scare me. I try them on. They never quite fit. I begin to feel self-conscious at my table for one, choking on my flawed perspective. My rational mind begins to overtake the rampant, raw emotions.

Okay, so I'm not the most pathetic person in the world. Darn! And you did bring me a beautiful bunch of wild flowers the other day. And you are the most patient person I know. And really, I enjoyed working cattle with you last week. You're a good partner and my best confidante and my true friend. And I'm not the easiest person to live with all the time. I know it's tough to make ends meet in ranching. It's just that I'd like to buy a jar of green olives once in awhile and not worry about how much they cost.

My red swollen eyes see the big picture more clearly now. My rantings subside as I begin the one mile walk home. The sun, calmly setting over the Black Hills, brings a close to this day. From a distance I see the dust swirling near our house. It's Marc and the boys returning from irrigating. Good. I'll run up the hill and fix a late supper.

They notice my red eyes and quiet demeanor and they know I've been on a Pity Party. I accept their extra hugs that night.

126

Shows

Let the gals handle it

For a number of years Marc managed a registered cattle herd for an accountant and his wife in Hillsboro, Oregon. Hank and Ellie often helped with haying and cattle work. Ellie faithfully brushed the cattle we had tied in the barn in preparation for the Pacific International Livestock Show held in early October. And she lent a hand on show day as well.

This particular summer it looked like a fourth cutting of hay would prevent us from taking the cattle to the show.

"Unusual year," Hank said.

"What about the show?" Marc asked. "We should take the animals."

"Can't. We have to get the hay in."

"I'll take them," I heard myself say.

"Yeah, you could," Marc said. "But you'd need help."

"Then I'll volunteer to help," said Ellie. "It's not that far away."

I must be nuts to bring this up, I thought.

"Do you really want to, Ellie? It's a lot of work."

"Rachel can be Ram Rod and I'll be Slave. What do you think, Hank? Can you find someone to fill in for me at the office for a couple of days?"

"No problem. I think you gals should go. It'll be fun," Hank said.

"That's settled. I'll help you gals load out tomorrow about 11:00 a.m., after I finish mowing."

Later that evening, having noticed the stricken look on my face, Marc assured me I'd do fine. "You've driven the gooseneck in Denver, remember? Can't be much harder here in Portland. Don't worry...if you have problems you can call Hank or me."

The next day I climbed into the driver's side, trying to do so with a confident air.

"I'll help direct," offered Ellie from the passenger side.

"Yeah, okay," I agreed as I swung the trailer wide out of the ranch driveway.

"Turn right. Straight through Aloha and Beaverton. I'll let you know when to turn left onto the cutoff to the four-lane."

I glanced over at Ellie. She appeared calm, though she was sitting a bit forward.

"You're doing fine, Ram Rod. Stay right. Then left through the tunnel and up onto the Freemont bridge. Watch for the Seattle signs."

I remained confident. The traffic wasn't too bad. As I stared at the overhead signs, the pickup and trailer moved a tiny bit into the right-hand lane. Honk! Honk! A fellow driving a small red sports car thought he needed more room.

"You keep the rig between the lines," said Ellie. "I'll watch for signs. Okay, good job. Now...turn right at the Marine Drive west exit that leads to the P.I. grounds."

Soon we were pulling up by the big barn.

"Good! Wait till I tell my mother what you and I are doing, Rachel. She'll never believe it! This will be fun," Ellie added with a delightful smile.

"Sure...right," I said, but I wasn't sure at all.

Ellie and I walked into the huge metal building and located the poster that showed a diagram of stall placements.

I watched efficient crews hauling cattle and show gear in.

"Here's Hank & Ellie Cattle Company," Ellie said, pointing to the middle of the poster.

"Let's see. Semmy's are in the northeast corner which means the Polled Herefords should be near the double doorway. Our area is two rows down past the middle alley and on the end near the wide center alley."

We checked out our location.

"Look at this humongous pile of sand, Ram Rod. Does someone spread this out for us?" Ellie stood transfixed, her eyes focused on the mound of wet sand.

"Yes. We do."

Ellie's arms hung limp. "Hmm."

I broadcast my cheery-having-fun face.

"You and I have to push the sand from here clear to the end of our area?" Ellie did not smile.

"Uh, huh." I didn't smile either.

"Straw. I thought you always bedded the cattle in straw."

"Fire hazard. And liability insurance. Besides sand is more comfortable for the animals. It's cooler."

"Oh."

"Let's go get the rakes and shovels."

Back at the livestock building. "I'll shovel the sand. You start leveling with the steel rake. Remember, we have to leave a bare spot for the tack box and chairs."

Ellie grabbed the rake. "Then can we go home?"

"Not yet."

We had shoveled and raked for a half an hour when we had a visitor.

"Hi, Rachel. Where's Marc?"

"Oh, hi, Ben. Good to see a friendly face." I leaned on the shovel. Ellie leaned against the tie up boards.

"Marc and Hank are haying."

"Haying. In October?"

"Unusual year. Late crop." said Ellie.

"Who talked you into coming?" Ben asked.

"No one. I volunteered." Ellie massaged her back. "But this will be fun!" She raked Ben's footprints from the sand.

"Sure, it will be." I said. I crossed my fingers behind my back.

"Right." said Ben. "By the way, I hate to be the one to tell you, but you just finished shoveling someone else's sand. When I read the poster it showed Hank & Ellie Cattle Company over there." He pointed two alleys away. "Can't believe Marc and Hank let you two women come here by yourselves. Call me if you need help." Ben sauntered off to his neatly groomed space, cattle tied in and laying down chewing their cuds.

"Sorry," I said.

"Yeah. Me too, Ram Rod."

We carried our tools to the new spot. "This better be right." Ellie shoveled furiously.

"I'm sure it is. Ben's never wrong about these things."

"Well, we're staying. No matter what."

We tossed our sweatshirts onto the dividing fence. Ellie heaved sand with the shovel. I smoothed with the rake.

"When do we eat and do you happen to have any aspirin?"

"Soon and yes."

There was more pushing, raking and shoveling until all the sand filled our space evenly.

"Okay, now a cold pop break."

"Whew, give me your aspirin. Have a couple yourself." Ellie wiped her sweaty brow.

"Believe I will," I said.

"Now what?"

"We have to haul in the tack boxes, feed and feed pans, water buckets, one of the hay bales, and the ranch sign," I explained as we walked out to the gooseneck.

"I sure liked our first spot, it was closer to the doorway. Are you ready? Let's head 'em up."

"Ready."

Ellie pushed the dolly while I steadied the large box. "Wanna trade?" I offered.

"No, you're too short. Short people steady and tall people push," said Ellie.

"What a sport!" I smiled.

We went back to the gooseneck for the next load. "We may as well leave the folding chairs in the trailer. We'll never have a chance to use them."

Two more trips emptied the pickup and trailer, except for cattle. I didn't have the heart to tell Ellie they had to be washed before they were stalled.

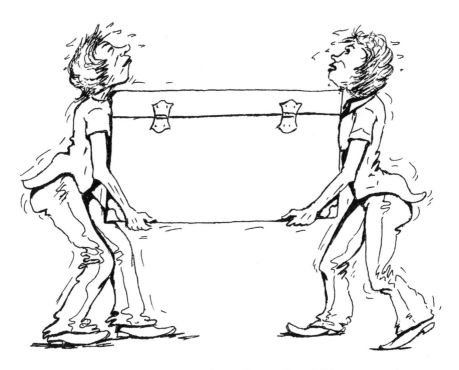

"See those two pieces of wood over there? We can use them for the uprights."

"Uprights?"

"To string the wire to hang the stall cards on."

We grabbed the wood. "Excuse me, that's my wood you two ladies are dragging off," a husky voice said.

We dropped the wood. "Way to go, Rachel." She winked. "I saw some wood outside the building."

"Perfect. Right diameter, but too long. Ask that guy in the Angus section if he has a saw we can borrow."

"Yes, Ram Rod. Anything else?" Ellie saluted.

I shoved the tack boxes in place and put the tool stand together. Ellie's search was successful. We measured and sawed.

"What a team. Hank and Marc were right. We can handle this." I said with renewed confidence.

Ellie looked in the tack box for wire. There wasn't any.

"No wire?" I repeated as if this would make it appear.

"No wire. I know...find some wire, Slave. Will do." She saluted again.

I continued organizing tack and writing names and birth dates of our animals on the stall cards. Ellie brought back enough wire to run the entire length of the building and back.

In no time at all we had the cards hung. Our stall was beginning to look like all the other ones in the building.

"Now, the ranch sign."

"Yes, I know. Tall person steadies...short person hammers nails."

"We're good," I said, hoping Ellie believed me.

Ben walked by. "You gals are doing a great job. Just think Hank and Marc will be sipping cold beer and you'll still be here. Say, I have beer in my cooler. Want one?"

"Be quiet, Ben. Reach up and tighten that screw on the cross board. And yes, we'd love a cold beer."

Ben climbed off the fence. "Here, let me give you ladies a hand hanging that sign. Looks like a heavy bugger."

Ben held the sign. Ellie and I clamped the hooks.

"Have you bedded your tie outs, yet?" he asked.

"Tie outs. Drats! I forgot all about them."

"I don't want to be a pain, but you might want to take care of that right away. There's a huge pile of trash down there. Looks like spaces are in short supply this year."

"Thanks. See you later. Come on, Ellie."

We hiked a quarter of a mile to the tie out area. Everywhere we looked there were cattle tied in or signs stating THIS SPACE RESERVED FOR....

"Darn Marc," I mumbled. "Wait until I get a hold of him."

"Can we go home yet? I'm hungry."

"Not yet. Soon."

"Look, Rachel, there's an opening."

"Do you mean by that cyclone fence a mile away?"

"That's it." Ellie actually sounded excited. She massaged her lower back. "I wish I'd taken more aspirin."

No wonder it was open. It took us twenty minutes to pull the long stemmed weeds and tramp down the grass.

"Are we having fun, yet?" I asked.

"Oh, sure," said Ellie. "You just keep the kind words flowing, Ram Rod. I thought we'd be on our way back home by now."

"Not yet. Soon, though."

"It's 4:30. What else needs doing before we can leave?"

"The barn is okay. We can finish up there tomorrow. That just leaves the cattle to be washed, blown dry, and tied out. Oh, yeah, and the feeding and watering. Shouldn't take too long."

"No wonder Hank agreed to my helping out. He's never done this before."

"I'll wash. Short people wash. Tall people operate blower. Is that okay?"

"Alright. Hurry up and wash one."

Ellie and I carted the wash equipment to the racks. This included wash pants, a gallon jug of soap, a hose, a scrubber, a blower, and two scotch combs.

When the two year old bull was washed, I passed the halter rope to Ellie. "Blow the hair up and forward, right?" she asked.

"Right. Hang in there."

An hour-and-a-half passed. The last calf was washed. While Ellie blew, I carried the wash supplies back to the gooseneck storage compartment and poured feed into five pans.

We rested our tired fannies on the tack box while the cattle ate and then walked the animals to the tie outs.

"Now, Ellie." I gave her a tired smile.

"We can go home?"

"Yep."

"Let's go! And wait till I get my hands on Hank."

We endured two whole days of routine work. Feed. Water. Brush. Scoop. Wash cattle. Dry cattle. More brushing and scooping. Lead cattle to the tie outs. Feed. Water. Drive twenty miles home. Fall into bed and sleep and drive back to P.I. in the early dawn.

On show day Ellie and I had the cattle washed and blown dry before Hank and Marc showed up.

"You've got them looking real good," Marc said.

"Thanks."

Hank slipped show halters on the animals while the rest of us applied all manner of goop to their clean hair, including foam, spray adhesive, and final mist.

Ben sauntered by. "What a great crew you have, Marc."

"The best," he replied. "I knew the gals could handle it."

The show was over in the early afternoon. Marc clamped his arm around me. "Hank and I have to be going. Numbers to crunch. Hay to make. Be sure to wash all the adhesive out of their tails and top knots."

"No problem. It'll be fun," Ellie answered, as she waved goodby.

"Do you want to wash and I'll dry?"

"No," Ellie said. "It's not good to change the system once it's running smoothly."

Ellie and I didn't break any records getting up the following morning. We scooped and brushed a little, visited with other ranchers and relaxed in the lawn chairs.

An hour before the 7:00 p.m. release hour, we pushed and steadied all the gear back to the gooseneck. On our second trip I heard foot steps behind us and a deep male voice said, "You two did a fine job this week. Do you hire out?"

I turned, then laughed at the tall, dark cowboy. "No, Ben, absolutely not."

"Well, maybe," Ellie joined in. "Rachel and I are pretty good at this now."

"NO WAY!"

The cattle eagerly stepped into the trailer. I snaked the gooseneck out through the crowded parking lot and onto Interstate-5.

"Thanks, Ellie. You did great."

"Thank you, Rachel, for acting as Ram Rod. Next time you be Slave and I'll be Ram Rod."

"Next time? Please re-phrase that, Ellie!"

"Oops, you're right. There won't be a next time. Hey, I'm famished. How about stopping at the pizza place? The one with the big parking lot?

Snakes

Until we moved to South Dakota, the scariest reptile I had ever seen was a garter snake. Though harmless, I had no desire to touch it or observe its habits. Live and let live was my motto.

But everyone knows that rattlesnake venom is poisonous. Before Darryl and Todd ventured out on their first exploratory excursion on our new ranch, Marc spelled out the rattlesnake rules. Never wander around the ranch alone. If a snake bites one of you, remain calm. Kill the snake if possible. Then the bitten one should stay put, while the brother runs for help. Always wear high top leather work boots.

Not thinking about snakes and leather boots, one day I walked to the corral fifty yards from our house to water the bulls. I shoved the water barrel closer to the hydrant. Then I heard the most frightening staccato of rattles echoing from the damp soil under the barrel. I jumped back just as an ugly head protruded from under the barrel.

I tried to yell, "Snake!" but I could make no sound at all. I peered down at my holey sneakers and a sick curiosity froze my feet in place. I had never seen a rattlesnake before, until these two three-foot long snakes crawled out from under the barrel into the open. Still terrified and speechless, I somehow unfroze my feet and ran like a banty rooster to the house. I was shaking so much I could barely grasp the car keys that lay amongst the junk littering the kitchen counter. But you can bet it didn't take me more than a minute to leap into the car and speed off to town where I bought a sturdy pair of water buffalo hide cowboy boots. The holey sneakers went into the trash barrel.

After this un-nerving rattlesnake encounter, I developed a sixth sense from observing their ways. I learned their patterns of sunning and denning. I increased my expertise in beheading the reptiles with shovels and steel fence posts and I could stun a rattlesnake with a rock hurled from 20 feet away. Admittedly, I nailed a couple of good rodent-killing bull snakes by mistake because their intimidating tail shaking and slithering body movement closely resembles a rattler. My survival instincts forced me to kill first and identify species later.

I nearly became accustomed to the sight of Darryl and Todd skinning rattlesnakes and gluing their skins onto an old barn board. And then seeing them displayed next to our wood stove in the living room. After viewing one snake autopsy that revealed a whole field mouse inside the snake, I nearly vomited right on the spot. "Boys," I said, "don't call me the next time!"

When Darryl and Todd didn't have time to immediately skin a fresh kill, they would coil the warm body, slip it into a plastic zip lock bag and freeze it. In my deep freeze, next to the meat and pint packages of corn and beans grew a collection of rattlesnakes. Though I knew the snakes were there, they scared me every time I lifted the freezer lid.

Early one afternoon, Marc laid down on his parent's lawn to snooze after a morning of cattle work and a filling noon meal. Darryl took a coiled frozen rattlesnake and placed it two feet from his dad's head. Then, he ran across the lawn and hollered, "Snake!"

Popping one eye open, Marc saw the rattler and leaped up so fast that Darryl began laughing out loud. "Joke,

Dad. Hey, just a little joke." Darryl ran his short legs off, trying to stay ahead of his charging father. He finally plunged into the irrigation ditch, leaving his dad at the edge shaking his fist and mumbling about tanning his hide.

Though we tried our darndest to decrease the rattlesnake population, we barely made a dent. We usually walked in a defensive, head's down posture as we crisscrossed the hillsides chasing cattle or irrigating.

Marc thumped each irrigation pipe before picking it up, just in case a rattlesnake was absorbing the inner warmth. And he always carried his short irrigating shovel, ready to slice and dice a darting head with the honed edge of steel.

One time Marc's concentration on setting the water overshadowed his snake precaution. He told us later that as he leaped across the concrete irrigation ditch, he caught sight of a coiled, hissing, rattling, shaking, rattler.

"I knew my foot would fall smack on top of him so I gathered up my adrenalin and propelled myself three more steps, landing on the other side of the snake!" Marc took a breath as though he was actually at the scene again. "Then, a quick quarter turn and I slammed the shovel down and watched a head roll to the side. I aimed another accurate slice and the eight rattles broke away from the damn critter!" As Marc's taut muscles relaxed, we clapped and cheered his bravery and skill.

Reptile respect, however, never evolved into a love of snakes for any of us. But respect from several close encounters with these poisonous beasts, did hone our powers of observation as we subconsciously remained alert to the where-abouts of the movers and shakers, as they slithered through the grasslands and river bottoms.

T
Tickets
Town support

Marc and I never considered paying our sons' speeding fines as part of the normal child rearing expenses. Periodically, we reminded Darryl and Todd that should they receive any traffic violation tickets, not only would we deduct the amount from their pay check, but we also had the power to revoke driving privileges for a long time.

"How long's that?" Darryl asked, as he leaned back on two legs of the kitchen chair, nonchalantly combing his blond wavy hair with his fingers.

"Don't tempt me," Marc replied.

Cultivating a town support group was critical to a successful outcome of our good driving campaign. Our spies—who to this day remain anonymous to our sons—were part of the neighborhood watch group set up by country parents.

One rare day Darryl drove the car to school. Reports began coming in from our town network even before he arrived home.

"Darryl," I said firmly that evening, looking up at him, "if you ever get caught driving that fast again, you can kiss your driver's license goodby."

"Mom, what are you talking about?" His 'who, me?' cocky grin giving him away.

"Eighty miles an hour may be your speed limit, but the law of the land says fifty-five."

"I wasn't driving that fast. What, do you have spies checking up on me?"

"Yep. Clocked you on that straightaway two miles from town."

"Boy, Mom, you're no fun!"

"You're right, and neither is excessive speeding."

Tools

His, mine, ours

My tools consist of one hammer and a combination phillips/regular screw driver. Not wanting to tempt Marc into swiping my tool, I hide the phillips end in the handle. If an inside-the-house job (like repairing the washer or dryer) requires that Marc borrow one of my two tools, I monitor their use. Then, before he escapes outdoors, I frisk him.

"Hey, honey, what are you doing...trying to hustle me?"

"Nope. Just making sure you don't walk out of the house with my screwdriver."

"What's the matter. Don't you trust me?" He winks.

Two screw drivers ago I trusted Marc. Now, I stand up for myself. I control the tools under my care. My hammer disappeared for a month and I had to make a trip to my secret hiding place in the nearby root cellar to retrieve my small hammer to pound a picture hook into the wall. When Marc wasn't looking, I nonchalantly walked back to the cellar and quickly returned the tool to its inconspicuous hiding spot behind the third row of dill pickle jars.

I am defenseless against Marc's lack of respect for not only my array of two tools, but also his insatiable need to abscond with other household items. Twice a year I bought brand new buckets, the kind used for scrubbing the kitchen floor, washing windows and cleaning woodwork.

The buckets would mysteriously migrate outside, never to return, no matter how much I pleaded or pointed out the lack of respect for one's tools. "Sharing," Marc responded with that innocent look, "isn't that what marriage is about? What's mine is yours and what's yours is mine."

"But once the bucket or broom or screwdriver falls into your hands, we quit sharing," I stated firmly. "And then I have to hunt all over the ranch to find my tools and my buckets."

Usually, my dear husband gets his hands onto my tools with pitiful arguments like, "The bull busted the gate. I have him tied up for now, but if I don't fix the gate right away, who knows what that crazy bull will do when he slips the halter and runs off down the highway, causing a serious accident with some stupid tourist and we end up getting sued for damages. Come on, honey, I need your hammer. I promise I'll bring it back today."

I hand Marc the hammer, repeating my oft-used line about being reincarnated as one of Marc's favorite cows. On the next trip to town I bought a half a dozen of those .99 cent screwdrivers and two of the three dollar 'on sale' hammers which I hid throughout the house.

And there was the time I actually allowed the hooked rug we bought when we were married, to do double duty as a blanket for the old Improver bull, who was suffering from pneumonia.

"Rachel," he said that day, "Improver's really sick. You know the fight he got into with the yearling bull in the pen next to his. Well, he beat up that bull pretty bad, but he's suffering from it. He's overheated and it's colder than the bejabers out. He's going to catch his death of pneumonia. Don't you have an old blanket or something I can cover him with?"

"I'm thinking..." I knew to what lengths Marc would go on behalf of the animals."

"Take your time. He'll be dead in two hours if we don't do something. He's old and hurting."

"Yeah, okay...remember that hooked rug? The one we couldn't use when we bought the double wide which had wall to wall carpeting? You won't wreck it, will you? We might need it some day."

"No, I won't wreck it. Where is it? Besides, is an old rug worth more than the bull?"

"It's on top of the rafters in the shop." I felt guilty. Marc was right. How could I possibly equate a bull with a hooked rug?

I prayed Marc would learn to care for tools the way his mechanical brother did. Marc cared about cattle, not tools. He treated inanimate tools differently. In his haphazard way, I think he believed in their eternity. That sooner or later they'd show up.

Or did he believe in the theory of replenishing? He planted tools all over the great stretches of prairie land under our care. Mostly they were left along fence lines, but once in a while a crescent wrench or a vice grips would pop up from where it had been planted when the pickup broke down in the middle of a pasture.

"Told you it'd show up," Marc said triumphantly, a smug grin creasing his face.

Marc planted tools as small as the chuck normally tied to the drill, to the large fence stretcher. We owned three fence stretchers in various stages of 'missing.'

Jerry-rigger Marc, ever the optimist, subconsciously labored under the belief that planted tools would reproduce if left alone along a fenceline. But they never did. Not one. He found a hammer, seeded three years ago when he was stringing a new strand of barbed wire. It was encrusted in rust, yet Marc cheered at the sight of his buried hammer.

"Aren't you disappointed that it didn't reproduce in all those years?"

"A little. Next time I'll locate a site with more fertile tool soil."

U

Udder Nonsense

Milk it for all it's worth

During the five years Marc and I dated, I assisted with many ranch tasks. Although I watched Marc milk the family cow hundreds of times, I was never curious to learn how to do it myself.

I listened, contently, to the lively zing and ping of fresh milk hitting the bottom of the metal bucket, while I fluffed fresh hay into the cow's manger and filled the water barrel.

I eagerly accepted the challenges of stick shift operation, learned correct cattle hair brushing techniques, and mastered the complexities of tractor driving. I discovered, however, that once proficiency had been achieved, one is NEVER able to unlearn a given skill. Well, one exception to that rule occurred during Marc's convalescence from wrist surgery. I did fix the stalling pickup each day by crawling underneath the engine to tighten a thing-a-ma-jig. I forgot how to repair stalling pickups the minute Marc claimed he was healthy enough "to do a little work around here."

Marc's sweet talking "you can do it," appealed to my pride. I enjoyed learning. He was a good teacher.

Never, however, did I let my guard down when Marc periodically asked, "Do you want to try milking her? Women are the best milkers."

"Oh, no thanks, dear...you do it so well."

Early in our dating years, my intuition told me that milking a cow was a chore I could always learn down the married road if I chose to. Marc didn't mind milking and I didn't mind not milking.

In twenty years of marriage I had never milked a cow. Nor had I any plans to ruin such a stunning record. But, neither had Marc planned to suffer from back spasms during the middle of calving season.

. Good Old Girl calved a healthy bull calf. Three days later, I told Marc that the calf didn't appear to be nursing and that Old Girl's udder looked full. Determining that she had a touch of mastitis, he suggested I milk the cow out. Get rid of the mastitis. The calf's not keeping up with her milk."

"Oh, no. I can't milk her."

"Sure you can. You can do it."

I hated those words. Besides, my stunning record was at stake. I couldn't give in now. "No way," I told Marc. "How about I pen the calf up until he's really hungry. He can deal with the mastitis."

"Nope. Wouldn't be good for Old Girl. She could lose a quarter..."

"So, she has plenty of milk in the other three."

"Sorry. She has to be milked. Mastitis could kill her."

"Go ahead. Lay the guilt trip on me."

"I'll come out. Where's my cane?"

"Oh, fine. Look pathetic. Go lay down. I guess I can give it a try." I moved my fingers trying to imitate the oft observed motion of Marc's hand. "Like this?"

"Yeah. That's it," he said, lying back down on the couch! "You got the right idea."

I walked slowly to the barn. Remember, stay close to her body. Less chance she'll kick you. Don't worry about the swishing tail. Go easy. Talk nice.

I lured Old Girl with a pan of grain close to the stout upright pole, eased a rope halter on and tied her fast. Good. That was a snap. "Hi, Old Girl. Just me here, going against my hard fought anti-milking plan. I've come to ease your pain. I clamped my fingers around the swollen teat. Hold still. Eat your grain. Squeeze. Work the fingers. One, two, three, four.

Nothing. Squeeze harder. She turned her head toward me. I hummed a lullaby. Rhythm, Rachel. Get a rhythm going. One, two, three, four. A wee bit of gunk plopped from the end of the teat. Yuck! She's making butter.

Bravely, I continued the squeezing until my wrist felt as though it were going to separate from my arm. A puddle of mastitis fluid collected on the ground. She was beginning to get antsy so I brought her a slab of alfalfa hay. More squeezing. More gunk. Finally, a semi fluid stream of milk hit the dirt.

I repeated this process, twice a day, for two more days. That bravery and a shot of LA 200 cleared up the mastitis. I immediately released myself from milking chores, and happily unlearned the milking skill. My record is still secure.

Varmints

One morning I awakened our elkhound's hunting instincts when I spied a large ground hog digging an underground den in my vegetable garden. Lacking skills with the shotgun, I ran into the house and grabbed the closest weapon I could find—the sponge mop—then made a beeline for the garden. I conked the furry critter on the head numerous times, until he lay still. He must have weighed thirty pounds. Shaking from the encounter, I went back to the house to finish washing the clothes.

About forty-five minutes later, after I hung the wet clothes on the outside clothesline, I grabbed the spade to bury the groundhog. Trouble is, he wasn't there. Alarmed, I backed out of the garden, wondering if he was perhaps hiding behind the pole beans, waiting to attack me. Feeling inadequately armed, I rushed to the house to fetch the elkhound.

Cappy's nose led him under the garden fence and into the pasture. I followed, carrying the shovel. Suddenly the dog bolted ahead, running fifty yards or so until he sniffed out the wounded ground hog. Feeling a bit guilty that I hadn't made a clean kill, I ran toward Cappy and saw that he was shaking the limp rodent by the neck. He dropped the dead groundhog at my feet then sat back in great pride, as if to say, "Look, aren't I a great hunter?"

Although Cappy's cattle skills were definitely questionable, when he took charge of predator control, he earned Marc's praise and respect. Ground hog holes were responsible for many injured legs of both cattle and horses.

The first evening of our arrival at the South Dakota ranch, all of us, including the dog, piled into the pickup for a tour of our new surroundings. We stopped on one of the bluffs overlooking the river bottom. Cappy bounded out of the pickup to explore his new territory, nosing wonderful new smells in the sage and choke cherry bushes.

Within minutes, we heard loud frantic yelping. Following the sounds we spied the dog and a large porcupine. Cappy turned towards us as if to say, "This ain't no groundhog!" Pawing at his prickled face, he wouldn't let us near him.

We finally coaxed him onto the tailgate and snapped a leash onto his choke chain. Marc's Dad called the vet who agreed to meet us at the clinic. Marc tried to hold Cappy steady so the vet could tweezer the quills from his face. Probably swearing to himself and cursing the newcomers, the vet suggested the dog be anesthetized. We attempted cheerful conversation for an hour while the vet pulled quills from Cappy's muzzle, lips, tongue, throat, and cheeks.

Two more porcupine tangles finally convinced Cappy he wasn't worthy of prey this difficult. Fortunately for us, he contented himself chasing field mice and occasionally succeeding. He loved his excursions with our sons as they tramped all over the ranch. And he always accompanied them on their hikes to the river to check the catfish lines.

Darryl and Todd would string a stout rope across the river and attach a half dozen lines to the rope. The cheese-baited lines netted enough catfish to supply neighbor Bill with all he wanted. Bill paid them a buck for each fish, which they saved toward county fair spending money.

Filled with entrepreneurial confidence, Darryl and Todd could barely wait for the real hunting season to begin in early winter when the value of raccoon pelts was at its highest.

"We're going to be rich," they bragged. They dreamed, schemed and planned their future life's work as hunters and trappers living off the land in the wilds of Alaska.

They were convinced that coon practice would test and hone their hunting skills. The two boys hiked many miles to seek out the best raccoon trapping areas. Applying grape jelly to the trap and ground to cover their scent, they hiked back to the house. Early the next morning they made their trap run before school. But it was empty.

"I told you, Todd," said Darryl, "coons don't like grape jelly."

Actually, I had suggested grape to keep them out of the strawberry and raspberry jam. Undaunted, the next day they took the dog with them. The elkhound smelled a raccoon immediately and captured him. The problem with this plan was getting the animal from Cappy before he had teeth holes all over the shiny pelt.

Knowing that either the cold weather or the dark morning hours would eventually discourage the mighty hunters, I kept my thoughts to myself. That is, until the morning of the honey can explosion.

Scared out of bed by a loud noise, I ran to the kitchen. Todd was standing over Darryl, washing his hair under the kitchen faucet. "What on earth is going on?" I demanded.

"Don't worry, Mom. We're fine. Boy, this honey sure is sticky."

Sitting on the electric burner was a quart tin of honey. "What were you trying to do! Blow the house up?"

"It was Darryl's idea," Todd spoke up. "I told him it was a dumb idea. That he should put the can in a pan of water..."

"Oh, shut up, Todd. That wouldn't have made any difference."

I looked at the stove knobs, the stove clock, and four burners—all covered with honey. "I guess you turned the burner to high, huh, Darryl?"

"Just to get it started. Todd and I figured the solid honey wouldn't work as well as liquid. How was I supposed to know the dang stuff would explode if you left the lid on!"

"Mom," Todd said, "don't sweat it. We'll make so much more money now that we've figured out the right racoon bait that we'll buy you a new stove!"

My bare feet stuck to the floor. I looked around more closely—honey on the loose everywhere. On the cupboards. On the light fixture. On the ceiling. "That's it! There will be no more hunting. I'm sick of the mess you boys make."

"We'll be glad to stay home from school and clean it up," they chorused in unison.

"Oh, no you won't," I replied firmly. "Wait, what's that in your hair? Here, Darryl, let me see that."

"It just got me in a couple of places. Ouch, don't rub so hard. I think I have third degree burns."

"I'll give you the third degree. Marc, get out here! How can you sleep through all this commotion!"

Darryl and Todd didn't get rich that winter. Darryl's couple of little burns turned into large infections and he had to give up wrestling for the rest of the season. I had to clip a bald spot to treat the more serious wounds and Todd lost interest in getting up at the crack of dawn to check racoon traps.

We shifted our attention to a smaller varmint. The chill fall nights triggered the holing-up syndrome, signaling all field mice within a half mile to make tracks to our double wide trailer. They scurried under the doors and through the insulation under the house. Once indoors they holed up in the kitchen and burrowed into any pile of clothes left untouched for twenty-four hours.

Now, it is true that I prefer the natural order of life and death. But when mice came into the house and proceeded to chew an assortment of household items and spew black droppings everywhere, I soon recanted my policy of no cats in the house. In came Explorer. I hid the dog food, hoping that hunger would improve the cat's motivation to hunt. It didn't.

I whisked the sleeping feline off the easy chair and set her on the kitchen floor where I'd just seen a mouse scurrying. "Over there," I pointed. "He went that-a-way." Ex remained unmoved by my plea. The mouse hurried into the drawer at the bottom of the stove.

"Sic 'em, kitty." She remained motionless. I pulled the drawer out, scaring the mouse into the oven. "Okay. That does it." I flipped on the oven light switch. There he was, searching through the crusted leftovers at the bottom of the oven. I snatched up the cat, opened the oven door and threw her in, slamming the door shut.

"Hooray," I yelled to Marc, asleep on the couch. "We, or rather the cat, finally nailed one of those nasty little rodents."

"Great," he mumbled.

In the end, the cat couldn't begin to keep up with the peanut butter and trap method, so I took over indoor predator control and left the outdoor varmints to Cappy and the outdoor cats.

Veterinarian Stuff

A question

Veterinarians are a special breed of men and women who attend college for years to achieve competency in the care of animals. And, in order to take care of animals properly, experience teaches them how to handle the owners, too.

After watching the vet pull a calf, our curious four-year-old-son once asked, "How'd that calf get in there?" Not wanting to give the birds and bees lesson, Doc said, "I don't know, Darryl, but he must have run awfully fast."

Vets learn when to laugh at or with an animal owner and when a more somber approach is necessary.

Weather

Too hot, too cold, too dry, too wet

The vagaries of Mother Nature offer topics for endless debate. Ranchers wake each morning with the same gnawing question. "What's the weather gonna do today?" Not, "What's the weather going to BE?" Do. Active, implying do to our crops, to our cattle, and to us, personally.

A few clumps of daisies growing wild in the pasture are eye pleasing. But when the pasture is full of daisies, we look on them as noxious weeds, crowding out nutritious grasses.

Weather's like that. Too much. Too little. Too hot. Too cold. Not so many days that are just right. The large snowflakes, falling gently from grayish skies, cause me to marvel and thank God for creating these geometric wonders. I straighten my arm to catch them on my the sleeve of my dark blue jacket. I look at the lacy shapes as they melt and go out of focus.

In half an hour the furiousness of the storm lays its whiteness everywhere, and the beautiful geometric snowflakes compact into a stinging reminder of the weather in the extreme.

Coping with the extremes of weather challenges the spirit and ingenuity of ranchers. Though we develop offensive and defensive plays in our weather game plans, we don't always come out winners. Mother Nature usually comes out on top. There are certain rules, however, that we try to follow to lessen the penalties of living in a harsh environment.

Too hot. When I wake up and the thermometer already shows eighty-five degrees, I begin the shut-down plan. I close the windows, pull the blinds, freeze more ice cubes, and call my mother-in-law to ask if we can hang out in her air-conditioned house, especially if the temperature reaches 100 degrees by noon.

Marc tried getting up at four-thirty, in the coolest part of the day, to irrigate, but his ability to tolerate extreme temperatures was greater than his desire to rise at dawn. So, after the noon meal and a nap on his folks' living room floor, I bravely offered to help with the afternoon irrigation. I figured I'd be shaded by the four foot tall corn stalks.

The heat was oppressive, and mixed with the humidity close to the ground, I discovered my lack of heat tolerance. Sun poison pimples broke out on my exposed skin. The front of my head throbbed and my stomach was near to regurgitating the cold roast beef sandwiches we had for lunch.

Marc assured me that it wouldn't take him long to set the 50 tubes along the parched soil of the corn rows. I laid back on the warm ground and tilted my baseball cap over my eyes until the heat pains subsided enough for me to walk to my mother-in-law's blessedly cool living room.

Coping with the "too much" of weather involves accepting one's limitations as well as understanding the physics of nature. During too hot summers, ranchers usually bale hay within hours of swathing. But, during extreme heat, if it's a job that can wait, we postpone doing it until late afternoon.

Too cold. It's too cold when...
- clothes stiffen before you can clothespin them to the line
- the laundry water drain pipe freezes under the house and stays that way till the spring thaw
- the 500 gallon water tank freezes solid and I have to freeze my butt off stoking the fire in a 50 gallon barrel that is supposed to thaw enough water to sustain the animals
- not only the 100 foot hose thaws and melts on the linoleum floor in the kitchen, but the brick floor under the wood stove is crowded with the tractor battery and the jug of oil drained from the tractor
- ears and tails of baby calves freeze
- tail switches of cows freeze
- Marc and I have to truck sale bulls to the vet's place, after hours, to wash them in warm water and dry them in a warm stall

- when peacocks die from hypothermia during the night

Too dry. It's too dry when...
- the grass crunches under foot
- alfalfa seeds don't germinate
- the gumbo soil cracks or the sand blows in cloudy billows
- the clothes dry at the bottom of the basket before I've had a chance to pin them on the line
- green sudan grass seedlings turn yellow and fall over
- stock ponds are muddied by thirsty cattle
- watering livestock entails a truck, a water tank, and a kindly neighbor with a good well
- a rancher has to phone the well driller

Too wet. It's too wet when...
- It's never too wet.

Too windy. It's too windy when...
- the laundry is scattered on the hillside below the house
- the john water is being sucked backwards and the pictures are jumping off the walls of our double wide home
- our slatted deck roof is carried in one piece up and over the roof of our house and lands in pieces on the south lawn
- the windrowed hay needs to be forked off the fenceline
- the center pivot is on its side
- the insurance agent suggests you buy an "Act of God" policy
- the tractor moves sideways and you're in a forward gear

Too much hail. There is too much hail when...
- one sees broken windows, dented vehicles, bruised livestock, slashed crops and pulverized gardens

Ranchers can boss spouses, children, pets and cattle. They cannot boss the weather. By becoming aware of weather's endless extremes, we learn to work with and around forces much greater than ourselves.

Y

Yucca

A p l a n t f o r a l l r e a s o n s

Beauty and danger are close companions, like the rose and thorn or the prickly cactus. One time Darryl and Todd decided as small boys, to test their survival skills. They planned to extract liquid from a cactus to quench their thirst and learn to eat the fleshy plant for sustenance.

With the seriousness of the great, historic adventurers, they first plucked the sharp barbs from the cactus. Without any further thought, they bit into the succulent plant. Immediately they sensed danger and pain. Teeny tiny, cactus hairs latched onto their tongues and into the soft gum and cheek tissue. The boys' survival experiment abruptly halted so their dad and I could tweezer the fine hairs from their mouths.

Darryl and Todd soon gained a respect for the indigenous plants and a thirst for research that didn't involve quite so much of the hands-on style learning.

It wasn't until Darryl graduated from high school, full of knowledge and wearing the armor of youth, that the danger of plants once again invaded his life.

The yucca, a member of the agave family, punctuates the prairie with its broad presence. The spiked stalks and bulbous pods, though crawling with stinging ants, alert the passerby to its stately beauty. Rattlesnakes and bull snakes scrape their changing skins against the coarse leaves.

Danger, however, lurks at the unmovable base of every yucca plant. Its 2-3 foot roots anchor it from outrageous winds, deep drifted snows, and careless dirt bike riders.

The summer our moratorium on NO MOTORCYCLES elapsed, Darryl returned from wheat harvest with a dirt bike. A mighty vehicle with a 500 cc engine. Roaring through the pasture, wind tearing at his blond curls, free from the long, tiring, dusty days of constant combining, Darryl felt like a caged animal just freed.

Catching air off an unmentionably high jump, Darryl flew above ground ending with a Chinese wheely, crunk, at the butt of a yucca plant. The mighty dirt bike stopped with a jerk, and hurled Darryl over the handlebars and onto his right shoulder. His dream of becoming the greatest dirt bike speedster of all time was cut short by the pain of a broken collar bone. Darryl learned that a mere mortal was no contest for the sturdy, indestructible yucca!

Z
Zoo

This ranch is one

My friend, Tammy, phones. "How's it going?"

"This place is like a zoo," I tell her.

"Busy, huh?"

"Yeah, it's crazy. I looked out the window this morning and there were 15 bull calves romping in the yard. It took forty-five minutes to chase them back to their corral and an hour to fix the fence."

"Not a bad start for the day," Tammy laughs.

"The hot water tank quit..."

"Is it the fuse?"

"Nope. Marc says that crud has built up in the bottom of the tank. He says we'll have to drain the tank and drag it outside to repair the heater elements."

"Oh my." This time Tammy doesn't laugh.

"And, you won't believe this," I say, "friends we haven't seen in fifteen years are due in today. Hope they don't mind cold water showers. And Todd—what a goof, he carved a five stitch slice into his finger last night. I told him to put a couple of AI gloves on his hand when he washes his heifer today."

"That's right, Junior show is next weekend, isn't it? Your place does sound like a zoo."

"Yeah, well, I gotta go. I hear Marc hollering outside. I better go see what the problem is."

So, I often think, what does it mean, "this place is like a zoo"? That we occasionally have a baby calf in the house? Or that our livelihood is derived from the care and feeding of animals?

I've walked through several zoos. Not one reminded me of my life on the ranch. A zoo's caretaker-to-animal ratio is far higher than ours and I've also never seen either wet or dry manure on a zoo worker's boots.

In fact, are there no messy places at a zoo? Is there a place for everything and everything always in its place? Pots of bright flowers adorn walkways all seasons of the year. I consider myself lucky if the bulbs I planted last fall rise out of the ground in spring and aren't blown over by strong winds or stomped on by cattle on the loose.

I don't think I've ever seen zoo animals cavorting about outside their penned areas. Except for a few pacing lions and tigers who don't look too happy, and a bored bear or two, most of the zoo animals look healthy and content. I bet the offices are tidy, too.

How I wondered, could I duplicate this life style so that when I say, "This place is like a zoo." it's a positive comment? And then the answer came to me.

Ranchers should form a Friends of Ranching association where we set schedules and supervise a volunteer cadre for:
- Candle light calving vigils.
- Trash patrols. At the ready following severe winds.
- Herders. The volunteers must have previous experience or attend a Friends of Ranching herding workshop.
- Hay and grain feeders and manure shovelers.

- Equipment handlers. To achieve this level of volunteerism, friends must pass the mechanics course which includes a session in jerry-rigging.

All Friends of Ranching will be entitled to sign up for behind-the-scenes lessons and hands on experience under careful supervision of Ranch Owners.

- Roping stationary steer skeleton heads
- Roping moving, breathing, live cattle
- Hay handling by the slab with the use of one's own hands (gloves provided)
- Hay handling by pitchfork
- Hay handling by tractor and farm hand
- Cow herding - active participant
- Cow herding - passive viewing from a pickup
- Clipping hair on cattle and other grooming chores
- Calving - must be available on short notice

Once a smooth running friends association has been established, Marc and I can devote our talents to developing intriguing brochures urging folks to donate vast funds to sustain our ranching operation. As a thank you for the monetary contributions we will offer unique and imaginative gifts.

DONOR CONTRIBUTIONS

$2.00	Bag of doggie treats
$2.50	One bovine pregnancy check
$2.50	One bale alfalfa hay
$7.00	One pair vice grips
$75.00	Gallon insecticide to kill a zillion grasshoppers
$100.00	One ton oats—enough to feed a dozen calves for one month

Donor Gifts
- Coffee mug stamped with the artist rendering of a Polled Hereford head
- Baseball cap emblazoned with the colorful Friends of Ranching logo

SPECIAL DONOR CONTRIBUTIONS

$189.00	Enough vice grips to station a pair at each of the twenty-seven gates on the ranch
$200.00	One year's hay supply for one cow
$325.00	A year supply of sunflower seeds to feed the birds of winter, who, during the summer months, perform as efficient insect eradicators

Special Donor Gifts
- Dozen beer steins, created by famous cattle sculptor Todd Remington
- The Grass Book, which includes 52 color photographs of grasses and noxious weeds

MOST SPECIAL DONOR CONTRIBUTIONS

$675.00	To purchase the number of peacocks necessary to eat a zillion grasshoppers
$1,000.00	Year's supply of vaccines required for a 100 cow herd health maintenance program

Most Special Donor Gifts
- The donor's name will be engraved on a brass plaque which will then be affixed to either a metal or wooden corral or pasture gate

EXTRA SPECIAL DONOR CONTRIBUTIONS

$1,500.00   Fuel to run haying equipment necessary to lay
             up feed to keep the animals from starving
             during the long winter months

$2,200.00   Genetically engineered high quality semen for
             the cow herd insuring survival of the species

Extra Special Donor Gifts
   • Larger engraved bronze plaque, to be placed on barn wall
     or in machine shop

UNIQUE CATEGORY CONTRIBUTION

$32,000.00   Diesel pickup with crew cab, 4-wheel drive,
              automatic transmission, cd player and four
              spare tires

Unique Category Thank-You Gift
   • A numbered, colored photograph, suitable for framing, of
     the ranch, taken at an altitude of 10,000 feet
   • OR a colored photograph, also suitable for framing, taken
     at close range of the donor standing beside the pickup

Since ranchers are listed in the Soon to Become Extinct
Species booklet put out by the Bureaucratic Government Statistics
Organization of Facts and Figures, I have no doubt about the success
of Friends of Ranching volunteers and the positive image evoked
when someone says, "This place is like a zoo."

Yes, I, Rachel, Do Take Ranching for Better or for Worse.

Rachel and her husband Marc,
continue to breed registered Polled Hereford
and Angus cattle in Oregon.

TO ORDER ADDITIONAL COPIES

Additional copies of *"Do you, Rachel, Take Ranching for Better or for Worse?"* are available.

Send:

☐ Copies @ $12.00 each $_____

Shipping and handling:
$3 per book $_____

Total amount enclosed: $_____

To:

_____
NAME

_____
ADDRESS

_____
CITY

_____
STATE   ZIP

Order from:

Rood Bridge Publishing
P.O. Box 1322
Hillsboro, OR 97123
(503) 648-9108